WHEN TWO LOVERS MEET

WHEN TWO LOVERS MEET

BRANDON LOMBARDO
Illustrator: Kayla Cameron
Photography.

Brandon Lombardo

Warning:

This book contains subjects that may be triggering or too graphic for certain individuals. Please talk to a trusted adult if you or someone you know is battling with addiction, self-harm, or having suicidal thoughts. By talking about these subjects and normalizing them it makes a world of difference for those struggling. Depression and anxiety can be debilitating, and from first-hand experiences, there are days where it can be very tough to have the energy to even get out of bed. Having a person in your life who you can talk to without feeling judged makes a world of differences. So I hope that I can do my part to touch as many people's lives as I possibly can to remind them of the potential they have, and how truly amazing they really are. Because every single one of us deserves a chance at happiness. So I encourage all of you to chase your dreams and to never be ashamed of who you are, or the things you've done.

About the Author:

If someone were to tell me three years ago that I'd be where I am right now I would have probably laughed at them. But taking a serious look back so much has really changed that I almost feel like I'm a totally new person. Being able to accept myself for who I really am and come to terms with my sexuality was a huge struggle of mine. It took me so long to even be able to say the words "I'm gay" out-loud. And that's why this book is so important to me because it's my passion. I wanted all the people out there that felt alone, abandoned, and unloved to know how much they really meant to me and to the world. We all have our own unique set of skills that we can contribute to society and even though you might be unsure of what that is right now it doesn't mean that there isn't a plan for you. We all have a purpose in life. If I had given up when I wanted to, I would have missed out on some of the best memories of my life. Most importantly though I would have never achieved my goal of writing this book and sharing the untold story of so many individuals in the LGBTQ+ Community. Because in some way or another I think we can all relate to one aspect of this book, some more than others, but nonetheless these things shouldn't be happening. Nobody should be put down for simply wanting to be happy. So remember to always keep fighting and no matter who tries to knock you down or discourage you, I believe in you and know that you have the potential to do so many great things.

Chapter 1

POV Connor

It all started on Saturday, April 13th. That's the day I met the love of my life. He didn't know it yet, but I knew that one day I'd marry him. The way he was standing in the corner acting all shy, I don't know how to explain it, other than love at first sight. His hair was a golden blonde with messy curls and he had on these super cute light faded ripped jeans. You could tell by looking at him that he was really sweet and that he didn't seem like the real rowdy type. He was very tense; standing there hunched over looking at the ground. Yet, you could tell he still had a sense of confidence in himself. I wanted to go talk to him but I was afraid I'd mess it up. I have a tendency to do that. I get all flustered and nervous and I start rambling on; over-sharing, and saying stupid stuff. Before I would even have a chance I would have already blown it. I remember thinking, 'what if he's the one and I just let him walk away?' God works in mysterious ways like that, so I decided to take a chance on this one. I had that gut feeling. I didn't know why, but this instinct coming from deep inside me was telling me I couldn't let him walk out of there without me. So, I took a deep breath, closed my eyes, and without putting any thought into it, rushed across the room towards him.

It almost felt impossible as I tried to get through the packed dance floor. Prying and pushing my way through couples that seemed to be glued together as they felt up on each other. I tried to be polite, but then it just came to a point where I had to shove people out of my way. Then, there I was, standing right in front of him. He was the kindest, sweetest looking person you could ever find, but somehow, I felt so intimidated. I was extremely nervous and I wanted to just crawl under a rock and hide. This was just so out of my comfort zone. I didn't do things like this; I was never the type of person to take risks. I'd normally sit back and think of all the ways it could go wrong. But, for once in my life, I had to take that first step, and there I was.

The lights were flickering rather quickly to the

beat of the loud music making it hard to see. He was a lot cuter up close. Not that he wasn't cute before, but now I could really see all of his features. I could see his perfect skin that seemed silky smooth, and that he had a small brown mole on the lower part of his face right between his chin and bottom lip. He had thin lips, and a butt chin, not that I was complaining. In fact, I found it cute. I found everything about him to be perfect. Even if I tried, I don't think I could have found an imperfection in him.

That's when my insecurities came in. How could someone like me talk to someone like him? What were the odds that he'd even like me back? Why did I think I deserve someone that amazing? I started to freak out, but right as I was about to spiral totally out of control, I was able to catch it. I held my breath for four seconds, then exhaled. I could feel my heart, which was almost pounding out of my chest, slowly starting to return to a normal pace. I just kept focusing on staying calm, repeating 'I can do this' over and over in my head. Then, without a second thought, while I still had the courage, I introduced myself.

"Hey, I'm Connor!" I said while thinking how cringy it was afterwards.

His whole face lit up, like he was surprised. I didn't know if that was a good thing or a bad thing, but I wasn't trying to think the worst.

"Alex," he said with one of the softest voices I'd ever heard.

There was an intense moment of silence where I didn't know if I should walk away, stay, or maybe ask for his number. I wasn't good with those things. We both just stood there awkwardly before he finally asked if I'd like to get a drink with him. I felt this rush of happiness I couldn't contain.

"Yes, I'd love a drink!" I shouted as he jumped back a little out of surprise.

We soon got to talking, and before I knew it, I felt like I had known Alex for years. We both were obsessed with pop music. In fact, we both were at the same concert in 2011. He was in row 210 and I was in row 215. Ironically enough, we both carried those same ticket stubs in our wallets, and we both agreed that it was the best concert ever. It was a collaboration between a whole bunch of pop artists. I mean everybody was there, it was like a mini Hollywood.

I'll never forget that night. It was a week after my birthday when my cousin showed up to my house and told me I needed to run an errand with her downtown. I didn't question anything, I just put my shoes on and went with the flow. We drove for about an hour before pulling up to the convention center where the concert was taking place. I had been asking for tickets since I first caught wind that they were planning the event, but my parents told me they were all sold out within seconds of the venue going live. My cousin even took a bunch of back roads to avoid raising any suspicions.

We drove around the outside and down the block before pulling into the parking garage. It was packed with cars, so we had to go all the way to the second to top floor. I still remember where we parked; floor nine, spot 354E. When I took off my seat belt, my cousin asked me to open up the glove compartment. I was a little suspicious by the way she asked me, as if she was anticipating something to happen, but I didn't think it was that. I thought it would be like a can of peanut brittle where something would jump up and scare me, but no. When I opened it, right on top of the black car manual were two white little ticket stubs. I didn't know what they were so she told me to pick them up and read them. I was still oblivious to what was going on, but as soon as I picked it up I lost it. I was so in shock, I never in a thousand years would have imagined that.

From the moment we got out of the car, all the way until we made it to our seats, I had the biggest brightest smile. Now whenever I become sad, upset, or I just feel off, I sit back and think about that night. I think about how free I felt, as I sat there in the crowd screaming my head off. I think about the rush I felt, as all of those famous people walked onto that stage, and I just totally lost control. It felt so nice to just let loose all the way, and to now know that Alex was there with me. It just kind of made it a little more special.

However, that was just the beginning of Alex and I's conversation. Once we really started talking, we learned so much about each other and how we actually had a lot in common. We both loved New York City; the noise and the buzz, always being able to see something new, and to be able to go on an adventure. His dream was to eventually get a studio apartment, so that at night, he'd be able to look out and see all of the flashing lights of Time

Square beneath him. What he liked the most about it was how diverse it was, and how different it was from what we were both acquainted with from growing up in the suburbs of New Jersey. I mean, the areas we both grew up in were very residential. Everywhere you went there were houses with occasional strip malls and gas stations. Nothing was open twenty-four hours, and all there was to do were the same three things. We agreed that for our futures, we wanted something different, new, and exciting. We were tired of this dull, boring life.

I immediately felt comfortable around him. Comfortable enough to where I was finally ready to ask the question. I mean, I was nervous, but I had to ask it. If not, it would have all been a waste of time. So, I paused, contemplating how to word it. There was no easy way to say it other than, 'are you gay?' Instantly, I felt regret. My heart started beating really fast, and I felt sick, but it was already said. All I could do was cross my fingers and hope that he was.

"Yeah, isn't it obvious?" he questioned jokingly.

When I tell you I nearly jumped through the roof in excitement, I nearly cried. I had spent the last three months getting out of this abusive relationship with this guy who wasn't ready to face his truth. He was confused, and that was okay, I was there for him. As a boyfriend, that's my job. But, it came to a point where he was bringing me down with him, and I couldn't do that. He said he loved me, but refused to come out or show any affection with me in public. We never went on dates because 'someone might see us.' We just spent most of our time together watching TV and movies in his basement.

Now, I'm all for coming out when you feel it's right, and I get that it's a difficult process, but I couldn't handle that much of an extreme. Every time I tried to break up with him, he'd cry and guilt me into staying. But finally, I had enough, and he took it really rough. He blamed me for all of his problems, and in a sense, I kind of felt responsible. So, after all that, I gave up on relationships for a little. To come out that night took a lot of courage, and for it to have worked out the way it did was like a miracle. I couldn't mess this up. This was my redo.

"No, I just wanted to make sure before I did anything reckless," I said.

"Reckless?" he questioned.

"Well, you know what I mean," I replied.

"Yeah," he said chuckling and then asked, "hey, what do you say we ditch this place and go get some fro-yo?"

"I wouldn't mind," I answered.

In about fifteen minutes the whole vibe had changed. We went from a loud club with strobe lights and tons of people, to now being the only ones inside of some frozen yogurt place, which was playing old school jazz music while the only worker there sat on his phone texting someone. I was trying to be mature and get something simple, so I went with cake batter topped with hot fudge and sprinkles. However, as I turned to pay, I saw Alex with the biggest cup the store had. He had filled it with all different flavors, and nearly every topping they had. It looked like something out of a first grade art project. The look on the cashier's face when he rang it up sent me over the edge, and I burst out into laughter.

If that were me, I would have died from embarrassment, but Alex wasn't bothered. He just casually pulled out his wallet as his yogurt started to droop and melt down the side of the cup all over the counter. The poor cashier tried to give him napkins, but there was no hope, it was a catastrophe. However, Alex handled it very lightly. He just laughed it off, where I would have been completely mortified.

I think that was one of the very first things I noticed about him; how he didn't care what anyone thought, he just did himself. Carefree, acting like nothing mattered. Truth be told, I spent a good portion of my life trying to please other people, and in the process, I missed out on a lot of great memories and experiences. Alex did what he wanted, regardless of who saw, or who cared. I mean, he was still shy and awkward, but he didn't let it get in the way of him being happy. That was something I needed to learn how to do because I spent way too much time worrying about what other people were thinking. I was at a point where I legitimately felt uncomfortable anytime I went out in public, because in my head, I stood out like a sore thumb, and I wasn't 'normal' like everyone else. It all stemmed from my insecurities in myself, and my lack of self confidence. Regardless of why I was doing it, I needed to stop. I needed to stop letting my anxiety and thoughts get the best of me, and I felt like Alex could teach me how to do that.

So, I just let go, and let him take charge. I followed his lead, almost like a dance, because clearly he knew what he was doing.

We were sitting down outside for a couple hours, long after the place had closed, and my anxiety was starting to majorly kick in. I mean, we weren't doing anything wrong, we were just sitting on a bench talking, but my brain was panicking. 'What if someone thinks we're trying to rob the place?' 'what if we get in trouble?' 'what am I doing here?' My leg started to shake up and down, as it does when I get nervous, and I started to get really hot, like I was burning on fire. My fight or flight kicked in, and I chose flight. I needed to get out of there, but I didn't want to blow my chance with him. I was at a crossroads, give in and leave, or stay? I knew if I left I'd regret it, and I knew if I stayed I'd be happy. It was just a matter of if I could handle myself and keep it in check for the rest of the night.

I think people have a terrible misunderstanding of what anxiety is really like. You can't just turn it off. Do you know how many times I've been told, 'stop your worrying,' or 'it'll all be okay?' The way they say it makes it sound easy, like there's some magic switch. Truth is, there are so many times that I wish I could just shut my brain off. There are moments when my brain gets so clouded with thoughts and worries that I'm bouncing from problem to problem, and before I know it, my whole head is just a jumble of mixed up emotions. I get everything confused, I can't think straight, and the more I try to shut it off and focus on the good, the stronger the thoughts get.

Anxiety isn't just as simple as everyone makes it out to be. It's actually exhausting. When you're out having a good time, out of nowhere, that little voice in the back of your head starts talking to you. 'They hate you,' 'they don't really like you,' 'you don't deserve this.' At first, it starts off like a little whisper, and you can ignore it. Except, the more you ignore it, the louder it gets, until it builds itself up and gains enough power to become a scream. Then, that's all you can hear, you can't focus on anything else because all you can hear are those screams telling you that you aren't good enough.

That's where I was with Alex. That voice was screaming so loud, and everything in me was telling me to leave, but I didn't want to. I wanted to stay, and be happy, and get to know him. I really did, but my heart and my brain weren't in sync. I had to do something, but I didn't know what. I knew the outcome if I left. I'd been down that path before. I'd walk away, go home, and then instantly regret it and realize it was a mistake. By the time I actually would have built up the courage to go back and correct the mistake, Alex would have moved on to someone else, and I'd be crushed by all the 'what if's?'

I knew what I had to do, I just didn't know if I could actually do it. I didn't think I had the strength in me, but I proved myself wrong. Every time a negative thought came into my head, I just kept reassuring myself, 'I deserve to be happy.' I know it sounds stupid, and at first it didn't seem to do anything for me, but I just kept telling myself over and over again, 'I deserve to be happy,' until finally, I started to believe it. As corny as it sounds, it actually worked. The voice was gone, and that little victory allowed me to enjoy the rest of my night with Alex.

I was able to actually listen to Alex when he was talking, and for the first time in a while, my thoughts were clear. I could actually focus on one thing without having to fight off the urge to just get up and run away. It felt great knowing that when Alex talked to me, I could actually pay attention and take in all of what he was really saying. I actually learned a lot about him. He liked to do at home DIY crafts, and he had this amazing creative side unlike anything I've ever seen. He showed me some of his drawings, and they were incredible.

My favorite was of two guys holding hands with a vine wrapping around both hands up the wrists leading to a rainbow heart at the top of their forearms. He said it was supposed to symbolize the strength of love in our world. All of his work had a symbol or meaning behind it, which gave him character and uniqueness. It made him passionate about what he did, and I loved it.

He had some self portraits in there that shocked me with the extent of how much detail he put into them. He knew how to shade them just right to give it a three-dimensional realistic look. He explained that each one of them stood for an important turning point in his life, and that when he was sad or down, he'd go back and look at them and remember that he had gotten through worse. His favorite was one he did of a tiger. It reminded him of strength and patience, and that those are two key things everyone must learn to master in life because life isn't easy. He explained that there will always be battles in life. Even when we're at our best, there will still be problems and we have to learn to be patient and strong, just like a tiger. The tiger doesn't overtake its prey by jumping out in an uncoordinated attack. Rather, it sits for hours, if not days, slowly tracking it's kill. It waits for just the right moment and then it pounces, and almost every time without fail, it gets the kill. Patience and strength put together can be deadly. Not just in a literal way, but in a spiritual way. It allows you to tower over the people who want to see you fail.

During all of this, I had noticed he was fiddling with his hands, but I didn't really give it much thought until he handed me what would have been the first gift another person had ever given me; an origami butterfly. To any normal person, they would have smiled and thought it was cute, but to me, it meant so much more than that. I wasn't the type of kid who had friends growing up that did nice things for me. I bought myself things. I did everything for myself. I never had a surprise party, or the experience of staying up until midnight on my birthday so that all of my friends could flood my phone with birthday wishes. I appreciated it so much that to this day, I still have it sitting on my nightstand, and every day I wake up and see it, I'm reminded of him and the impact he had on my life.

I obviously thanked him, making sure he knew how much that meant to me, and then came my turn to share.

"So how about you? I've spent all this time talking about me, what do you do for fun?" Alex asked.

Now what could I possibly say to follow all that up that wouldn't make me sound like a total loser? I'm not good at anything. I mean I write and stuff, but other than that I don't do a lot with my life. I didn't want to lie, but I didn't want to come off as this dull guy who doesn't know how to have fun.

For the first time in my whole life I decided that I'd just be myself. I'd be the person I was meant to be and I'd let the rest of it take care of itself. If Alex hated me and thought I was boring then so be it. Maybe the reason I was always getting hurt in life was because I never was comfortable enough with myself to actually live life. I spent every moment trying to be this person I wasn't; a person who had a million friends and a thousand memories.

I hated my life and I wished I could just erase my whole past. I hated that my life wasn't normal like everyone else. What I was doing was trying to lie to myself by telling these fake stories. I was hoping that maybe one day I'd believe them myself. Sure, the people around me may have believed me when I told them all these crazy far fetched tales of how I had a ton of friends and I did all these interesting things, but I knew that was a total lie.

I needed to wake up because that wasn't the reality. The reality was that I was broken for as long as I could remember and I didn't know how to handle it. I didn't have friends, or a life. I'd spent all of high-school playing video games in my room with a bunch of strangers I met online. I never had a serious relationship or anything like that. I never went to a party or a football game. I never even went to the mall on the weekends or the movies on a Friday night. All of this bothered me, and I hated it, but in that moment I realized something. I could never change my past; it was done and over with. All I could do was prevent my future from being the same way and it started with accepting the fact that all of those things, good and bad, are what makes me, me. I couldn't act like they didn't happen, because they did. All I could do was ensure that I didn't continue the cycle, and that started right there with Alex.

Chapter 2
POV Alex

I didn't want to go to the club that night, in fact, I almost turned around twice while driving there. Clubs bothered me, I hated being around large groups of people like that. As a gay guy who's very open with my sexuality, my life hasn't been easy. High school was a nightmare, and after that, the real world wasn't any better. All the people who'd curse me out on the street, the people at my job who'd judge me for my appearance or how I talked and acted, it got to be a lot.

Now, I've never been one to be fake, even with myself. Being gay was who I was, and I wasn't going to not be myself because some straight dude in a pick up truck doesn't like my little pink car. I wasn't going to stop wearing skinny jeans because my manager said that I had to 'dress like a man,' or I'd get fired. Nine out of ten people who came into my life tried to control me and tell me who or what I should be, and I hated it. I was different, and nobody could ever see that. They all tried so hard to try and make me 'normal,' but that just isn't me.

I speak my mind. I'm not the person who sits there and fakes a smile acting like everything is okay. If you're doing something I don't like, I'm going to tell you. I'm not some wall flower who's gonna sit there acting pretty. I'm going to do what I want, when I want, regardless of who gets mad. That is why I didn't want to go out that night, because after a while, I started to get tired of it. The whole world wanted to change me, and I began to think I'd be better off on my own.

I felt more peaceful when I was home. I'd stay in my room all night drawing and painting. I love to draw skylines, especially New York. I've had a fascination with the city since I was a little boy. I'd watch the ball drop on New Year's Eve and I'd be so jealous of all the people down there who got to see it in real life. I loved the idea of it. It was different, but in a good way.

Everyone and everything was different.

I lived in the suburbs where everyone had the same two story house with the same white picket fence, and they all had the same little nasty Chihuahua that would bark at you while you walked by. Everyone's dad was a Lawyer or a Doctor and their moms stayed home cleaning and baking all day. I never wanted that for my life. I want something more. I want my life to mean something. I don't want to just be your ordinary citizen. I want to grow into something, to help someone, and change their life. I want to be the reason someone smiles, because I know what it feels like to not have anyone in your life and to always feel misunderstood. I want others out there to know that they aren't alone, because that night when I walked into that club, I was at rock bottom.

I walked into that club with the mindset of getting black out drunk in an attempt to drown my pain, but things didn't exactly go as planned. I was standing there waiting for the bartender, and I remember thinking how stupid the whole concept of going to bars to find guys was. What were the chances that a halfway decent guy would be out dancing in a club at midnight. That stuff only happened in movies and books. It was stupid, love was stupid. If I'm being totally honest, I didn't even believe in true love, and then I saw Connor.

Here was this giant guy, I'm talking like 6'2, two hundred and ten pounds. His shoulders were huge, he had humongous biceps, and he looked like a total gym buff. Yet, there he was, trying to hide behind a pole so that I couldn't see him checking me out. I remember thinking to myself, 'what an idiot,' but in a good way, not like a mean demeaning way. It's like when they say that elephants are afraid of mice. It was so unlikely that someone like him, someone attractive, someone who could probably be a model, would be scared of me. Of me! I was like two seconds away from going over and telling him he needs to do a better job at hiding when he started walking over.

At first, it was awkward. The conversations were weird and slow, and they felt forced. We were both extremely nervous and trying not to screw up or say the wrong thing. Then, we started talking about our favorite musicians, and from there it took off. We talked about music and our futures. We talked about our dream trips. He wanted to go to Egypt and visit the Great Pyramids. He was a total history nerd. He chewed my ear off for about twenty minutes talking about Alexander the Great and some other mumbo jumbo that was too boring to listen to, but I loved his passion. I loved how intense he got about the things he loved, how he knew all these little details. I'd hope he was the same way in a relationship. 'Relationship?'

I couldn't believe it. Did I actually like him? Was I actually falling for someone? Normally, in all of my past relationships, they all made the first moves and threw themselves at me while I would play hard to get. But this, I'd never felt like this. I mean we seemed compatible, we had a lot in common, we both had a mutual interest in the other. I think I was catching feelings.

I felt an attraction to guys before, but I never really felt love like this. Now, I know I only knew Connor for like an hour, but I just loved everything about him. He had this way about himself that I couldn't get over. He was naturally funny, there were so many times he made me laugh and didn't even try. He was caring, and tentative. I could tell that he actually meant what he said. He wasn't the type of person to ask how your day was just because. No, he actually cared about how your day was.

The way he'd make a half smile and laugh at his own jokes was so cringy, I couldn't help but fall in love. This was the first time in my entire life that I had feelings for someone. Every guy I dated was hot, and there was a physical connection, but nothing else. We didn't vibe or connect. We never had anything in common, besides thinking the other one was attractive. With Connor, it was so different. I actually wanted to get to know him. I wanted to make memories with him. I wanted to watch movies together and laugh. I wanted to be happy together.

I suggested we leave the party and maybe go somewhere more quiet where we could actually sit down and talk. So, we went to this fro-yo place and we started to talk about each other. We talked a lot about me at first. I told him all about my crafts and my projects. I showed him some of my new ideas, and some of my more complicated pieces. When it came time to talk about him, he hesitated. I didn't want to push, but I figured that this would be the part where it was all too good to be true. Where he'd tell me he was a sexaohlic, or that he was a serial killer. I didn't know what, but I knew he was hiding something. I could tell from the way he changed. At the club, he was so open and I couldn't get him to shut up. Now, when it came to his personal life, he gave me one word answers. I was about to get up and leave when he finally spoke.

"Look, I'm not gonna lie. I've been through a lot of stuff in life, and I've struggled my whole life to get to a point where I'm okay with it, and I'm still not there yet," Connor began. "Truth is, I've never had any friends, I've never had a best friend, or even so much as one person who genuinely cared about me. I mean, I did before I came out, but once I did, they all left," he paused. "So, I'm not gonna lie and act like my life is filled with these amazing stories and that I do all this crazy stuff because I literally spend my weekends laying in bed writing and reading," Connor finished.

At that moment, I knew he was the one! The reason I broke up with everyone of my ex's was because none of them could be honest with me, they all wanted to be pretty and perfect. Honesty is hard, but it's essential. Without it, there's no trust. I knew it wasn't easy for him to open up to me like that, but at least he did it, and it made me ten times more attracted to him. I saw in him someone who knew they needed to change and actually had ini-tiative to want to do better. He could've given up and been home that night playing a game or sitting in his room alone, but he took a chance. Instead, he was there with me, which was uncomfortable for him, but he was doing it, and I liked that.

When I thought about my future, I always saw myself with someone who was filled with courage, someone who wanted to be the best version of themselves and would never give up. I saw myself with someone filled with passion and hope, who knew that even on their darkest days, it would get better. When I looked into Connor's eyes, I could see that in him. I could see the pain as he held back tears talking about his past, and I knew that feeling all too well. So I did something I never thought I'd do. I opened up to him.

Chapter 3
POV Diamond

As Alex's best friend, I saw him at some of his darkest times. I don't mean like when he got drunk at a party and needed me to hold his head up while he vomited. No. I mean like some very serious life changing traumatic stuff. Alex tried to kill himself his junior year of high school. I was the one who talked him down. If it weren't for me, Alex wouldn't be here right now.

It all started when he met Zach. Zach was poison to Alex. Alex craved attention and popularity all throughout high school. Being the shy quiet kid that nobody noticed he had no friends besides me, and he hated it. No matter how hard he would try to make acquaintances he'd always get shunned or ignored. Because truthfully if you just looked at him you would think he was a total weirdo. I mean he always had his hair dyed bright colors, and he had his septum pierced along with his tongue. He always wore odd clothes that most people would consider 'ugly' or unfashionable', but that's just who he was. You really had to get to know him to realize what a sweet, genuine person he truly was. So when Zach started bullying him, Alex didn't say anything because at least now someone was finally acknowledging his existence.

Suddenly all the popular kids noticed him. The football players, the cheerleaders, even the stem kids all knew who Alex was. Now, none of them knew he was gay, or anything else about him other than the embarrassing things Zach told them. Like that his family was poor and they didn't have any money. He told everyone that Alex was ghetto, and would always find ways to embarrass him whenever he had the chance. One day Zach opened his locker right as Alex was passing by "accidentally" hitting him in the face. There was another day in the cafeteria where Alex was wearing a white t-shirt and from the table behind him Zach and his friends flung ketchup packets at his back staining his shirt red.

I used to get so mad at Alex for letting Zach get away with it, but he loved the attention. He didn't want to go back to being the shy quiet nerd who nobody talked to. So if that meant the whole school laughing at him, at least now he was getting recognized by someone.

For one of the games the football team convinced him to wear the mascot costume. and because of this the attendance nearly tripled. But once again, this was all really bad because those people in the stands chanting 'Alex! Alex!' weren't supportive. They were all mocking him, and the twisted part about all of it was Alex really thought they were his friends.

Eventually Alex opened his eyes, but it was too late. Even though Zach still made fun of him, I could tell Zach cared about him. Because when things got really out of hand, he actually did try to fix it and make things right. He tried to change the subject, he told people to stop bothering Alex, but Alex had become the school laughing stock; his name wasn't going to be silenced that easily. He'd get tripped in the hallway, papers thrown at him in class, one day they even slammed his backpack on the ground shattering his computer. Alex was stuck, and he didn't know what to do.

Zach felt more guilty than everyone. He never showed it, but I could tell. Zach had no real reason to stick around, but he did. He'd warn Alex if the other guys were planning something, and they still texted on a daily basis. Except now, Zach was talking like a real friend, his whole outlook changed towards Alex. He apologized and was trying to make it right. Zach was still selfish though, and he never was public about his friendship with him. In fact, Zach would turn his head in the halls when he saw Alex, and if he couldn't avoid it, he would join in with the others. All because he cared too much about his reputation than to worry about what he was doing to Alex.

I swear, Zach was some sort of wizard or something because he had this wrap around Alex. It was unlike anything I'd ever seen. No matter what Zach did, Alex never got mad, he always forgave him. Alex really thought they were best friends, and I think deep down Zach wanted to be, but he wasn't ready to give up his lifestyle for that. He knew being friends with Alex would mean giving it all up. All the friends, and all the parties, all of it gone.

Then one day, it all clicked and made sense. I figured out why Zach cared about Alex, and why Alex kept defending him. The two were in love. Now, Alex denied this for the longest time, but he couldn't lie to me. I knew him too well, and like all lies, the truth eventually came out. Except, I wasn't the only one who found out. Someone allegedly saw the two at one of the parks on what appeared to be a date, and Zach, in fear of losing everything, lost it. He blamed Alex, told the whole school Alex was gay and tried to make a move on him. And when Alex tried to defend himself Zach punched him the face and called him a 'faggot' in front of everyone. Alex was stunned, and he didn't know what to do so he just got up and scampered away.

I'll never forget watching that and being so angry as everyone laughed at what just happened. How was that funny? I was so upset I wanted to cry, but I had to keep it together and find Alex. I was searching everywhere and finally I found him curled up in a ball crying under the bleachers. He told me that Zach threw himself at him and that he didn't even want to at first. He told Zach no a million times but Zach was persistent, and eventually Alex gave in. Zach forced Alex to have sex with him, and forced him into a relationship. If anything it should have been Alex slugging Zach in the face.

After the fact Alex tried to forget the whole situation but everyone made that extremely hard to do. The guys came up with a game called the 'gay touch' similar to the cheese touch, but instead if you touched Alex it would make you gay. So every time Alex walked down the halls everyone would jump away from him, and some guys would try to push their friends into him, just so that their friends could lose the game. It was sickening to watch this all happen, and see Alex be humiliated the way he was.

Alex was trapped, he was still in the closet to his parents so he couldn't get help. If he had gone to counselor they surely would have told his parents, and than what would he have said, 'Hey mom and dad, I'm straight but the whole school thinks I'm gay?' He had no help, so he turned to drugs.

I didn't know how to help him. I kept trying, but every time he got high he lost a little bit of himself. Eventually, he turned into this whole new person; this monster. He would do anything to get high, even if it meant hurting the ones he loved. He pushed me away and blocked me out, but I kept trying. Finally, I walked away and I told him that when he was ready I'd always be there for him.

Six months later I got a call at four in the morning from him. He was ready to talk. I snuck out my window and biked halfway across town to this old bridge covered in graffiti. Nobody was around, and the only thing I could see was the shadow of a homeless man hunched over sleeping on the ground with a ripped hoodie. I called Alex and I heard his phone ring; it was him. He was the homeless man. He had lost about twenty pounds, he was all drawn and skinny. I could see his neck bones. He had a shaved head and his arms were covered in needle marks. He handed me a note.

It read:

I can't handle it. I can't handle living like this. Every night I go to bed praying to god that he takes me in my sleep. Every morning I wake up mad that I'm still here. I want to die. I don't want to be in pain. Please don't feel bad or upset, this is what I want.

"Give it to my parents," he said.

That's when I noticed the pills in his hand. I wrestled him to the ground, he had no strength to even fight me back. I could tell he was trying to use all his strength to get me off of him but it was no use. He was too weak.

"What are you doing? Let me die!" he screamed.

He was hurting but I knew that he didn't want this. He was desperate for a solution to his problem, but death wasn't it. He may have thought it then, but I knew he wasn't put on this Earth to just die like that. He was too sweet and kind. He had so much to offer to just throw it all to waste. So, I made the hardest decision of my life and I called the cops on him. Because of me, he was sent to an inpatient facility and was forced to get help. He hated me, but I was okay with it. At least he was alive.

Chapter 4
POV Michelle

My whole life I've struggled with my weight. Never being able to wear the clothes the other girls did. Never being able to take cute pictures because I felt like I was too fat and people would think I'm disgusting. It got so bad to the point where I would turn on the shower and wait for the water to steam up the mirror before I took my clothes off, just so I could avoid seeing myself. I hated who I was. I literally would have done anything to change it. You can escape an abusive relationship, or a toxic best friend, but you can't escape your thoughts. I was stuck everyday, constantly thinking on repeat 'What can I do to get skinny like the other girls?'

I looked into exercise routines and these special diets. I tried going vegan and Keto. I started running, but I wasn't seeing the results, not like I wanted them to be. Yeah, I felt better, and maybe I lost a couple pounds, but that's not what I wanted. I wanted to find a way to lose all my weight in a matter of weeks, not months. I'd watch all these online videos and they'd say stuff like 'By the end of the year you'll be looking brand new!' or 'In just a matter of a few months you'll be a new you!' Who wanted to wait that long? I couldn't handle it, so I decided to hardcore diet.

I stopped eating all carbs, and anything with sugar, and when that didn't work I started skipping meals. At first, it was just having one less snack. Then, I started missing breakfast. From there, it was lunch and eventually dinner. I got to a point where I ate one meal every other day. It was rough at first, I was so hungry, but I had to push through. Every time I thought about eating, I'd go for a run or I'd take off my shirt and look in the mirror to remind myself of what I would be giving up if I gave in and ate. I kept pushing myself when I knew I couldn't handle it, but it was my only choice.

I grew up overweight and I stayed that way my whole life. I had nothing but bad memories that came with it. Not being able to share clothes with my friends, always seeing clothes I loved but never finding them in my size. Looking back at pictures from my birthday or an old party and wanting to be sick at how big I was. Not being able to play sports, or feel comfortable in my own body. It all got so much and I refused to deal with it. I just wanted to be happy. I wanted to be like my friends, and everyone else. I was disgusted and I didn't care.

As I kept going with it, the worse it got. I used to get really sick, these headaches unlike anything I'd ever experienced. The whole room would start spinning and my head would start pounding. I'd get really weak and a wave of tiredness would come over me. My eyes would get really heavy and I'd feel my legs almost give in, but I didn't care. I kept pushing. I kept trying because I wanted so badly to change and I didn't know what to do.

I eventually got to a point where I was just vomiting everything I ate, and then one day, it all caught up with me. I was laying in bed and I got really hot, then I started sweating like an intense marathon runner. I got up to get a bottle of water and just collapsed. When I woke up, I was in the hospital. The doctors were confused about what happened. I guess they'd already done a bunch of tests and they couldn't find anything wrong. They asked me when I last ate because my blood sugar was low. I knew if I told them the truth, I'd get labeled as crazy or sick, but if I lied, who knows what would have happened.

I had no choice but to come clean, so I told them everything. I told them how it all started, how I hated who I was and I wanted quick results. How I was going crazy trying to lose weight, and finally, I snapped and I resorted to this because this was what worked. Well, after spilling my guts for about a half hour trying to convince them I wasn't crazy, they finally sent a psych doctor into my room and we talked just the two of us.

We talked about a lot of personal stuff. He asked me questions like if I ever used drugs or alcohol, or did I try to kill myself. All these ridiculous questions that had nothing to do with what I was saying. I guess it was protocol, but it was pissing me off. I wasn't some troubled child who was abused or something. I didn't need a psychiatrist. I wasn't sick, or so I thought.

When he told me I had an eating disorder I burst out into laughter. At the time, I thought I had it under total control, but now I know I didn't, and I know if it weren't for that doctor, I'd probably have gotten really sick and who knows what could have happened. But at that time, I was so mad I didn't see it as that. I saw it as him attacking me. I took it personally when all he was doing was his job, but when you're in a vulnerable state like that, you tend to lash out at others. Especially the ones trying to help you. I'd spent weeks trying to tell myself that I was enough, and my weight didn't define me, but I couldn't get past it. All I saw myself as was my weight; two-hundred and ninety-five pounds. Whether I was willing to see it or not, I needed help.

The psychiatrist said I needed to spend time in a facility for young adults struggling with depression, anxiety, and other sorts of things like that. It was supposed to be extensive therapy with peers going through the same problems as you. When I found this out, I had to be tied to the bed because I was so enraged. I didn't think I needed it, I was fine. I just needed to lose a few pounds and I'd be okay. I had come such a far way for it to end like this. I'd lost twenty pounds so quickly, in my eyes what I was doing was working. I didn't care that I could barely eat half an apple without gagging, because that was normal to me. I was used to it, and the concept of eating full meals didn't feel normal.

I didn't see what a real problem any of this was until way after the fact.

When I got to the facility, I was taken out of the ambulance and I got to say goodbye to my parents before I was admitted. The first two weeks I wasn't allowed any visitors. If all went well, then I'd be allowed to see my parents. I remember looking in my mom's eyes as she tried to play this tough role, which I could see right through. I could see the sorrow, and the guilt in her eyes. All I wanted was for her to know this wasn't on her, but I didn't know how to say it. My dad was a man of steel. I'd never seen that man cry a day in my life, and I still haven't, but that day must have been rough. He grabbed my shoulders, looked me in the eyes, and said "it's gonna be fine baby girl, you've got this." He kissed me on the forehead and then hugged me. He hugged me so tight I nearly felt my eyes pop out of my head. At that moment, I made up my mind. I was going to leave this place, and make it up to them.

After I was admitted, I was given a mini tour of the place. It was no Five Star Hotel, but I'd seen worse places. The other kids seemed to hate it as much as I did, but I wasn't expecting any different.

There was a rec room, a TV, and a couple books. They had these worn out bean bag chairs that sat on the ground like sad lumps untouched by anyone. They had an office, a nurses office, and several different therapist rooms. Then, I was brought to my room. This little shoe box that made the hospital look like a palace. The nurse left me to settle in, but what a joke that was. They wanted me to call this place home? Never. I mean, I didn't have a window, I had this thin mattress and a bed frame that squeaked every time I moved. One dresser with three draws to put all my belongings in, and a paper pillow case. I felt like I was in a war.

That night I consulted with a dietitian, she was a total waste of time. She talked to me about 'the importance of eating,' as if I didn't already know that. Then again, if I did know that, I wouldn't have starved myself for a week straight. She talked about the food groups, and the food pyramid. How important a balanced diet is, and she told me that they would give me a normal size meal, but that I should only eat what I felt comfortable with. I shouldn't rush into overeating because I'd get sick. So what did I do? Exactly the opposite. I got so sick, it was the worst feeling ever. I hated that place so much, and I thought that by rushing the process and acting like I was 'normal' would get me out sooner, but I was wrong.

I hated that place because we like to believe that we're doing all the right things for all the right reasons. We hate to give ourselves wrong, and at some point, it just turns into an ego game. You've told all these people you were okay and you didn't need help, and now you feel like you can't take that back, so you keep trying to fight a fight you know you're going to lose. That's where you give in and start to see it as a goal rather than a problem, and you just live it. Talking in therapy and being there forced me to realize that I, in fact, did have a problem, and I needed help, and I hated that. The only one other person who hated it there, more than me, was Alex.

Chapter 5
POV Alex

I hated that place, it was like prison to me. To be fair, I hated everyone and everything at that point. I hated my parents for not seeing that I needed help, because in my own ways, I did tell them. Every time I made a joke about dying or I'd say 'ugh I don't care anymore,' they blamed it on an overload of school work or some other typical high school stuff. The thing was, I was reaching out for help. I was too afraid to just say it out right because, let's be honest, how many of you would be able to walk up to your parents and say 'hey mom and dad, I think I want to take my life.'

I tried to do that, and I just couldn't. I had all these thoughts running through my head, 'would I be called crazy?' 'would they even believe me?' Now, this was before I ever actually seriously considered taking my own life. In the beginning, I just kind of thought about it a lot. I'd have a bad day and say 'man I wish I was dead,' and I'd sit there thinking about how peaceful my life would be if I wasn't around. I'd sit there for hours thinking about how much happier I'd be. I knew I had a problem, but I didn't know how to get help without ruining my whole life.

There is such a bad stigma around suicide. You can't be alone anymore, everything you say is taken so literally. You're not allowed to joke or mess around. You can't be trusted with even a plastic knife. These are all things I want to change because, in all honesty, most people don't talk about their suicidal thoughts for all those reasons, and neither did I. I didn't want to put myself in that position if I didn't have to, and at the moment, I had my thoughts under control.

And I was doing good, until one day i just completely gave up, and I started getting really reckless. All of it was just a cry for help. Behind all the 'I hate you,' and 'I wish you weren't a part of my life,' were pleads. All I needed was one person to say 'hey, you've been acting strange lately, you okay?' That's all I needed, but it never happened. So when I finally did do it, I blamed them, because maybe if they would've helped me then, it wouldn't have gotten to that.

The thing is, I could have had anyone talk to me, and no matter what anyone could have said, it wouldn't have changed my mind. Would it have prolonged it? Maybe. But at the end of the day, eventually, I was going to do it. I didn't want to face the truth, because the truth was ugly. Have you heard the saying 'the truth will set you free?' It makes the 'truth' sound like this marvelous thing. When I think about my truth, I see an empty void filled with negativity, and self consciousness . But that's my truth! And it wasn't until I accepted that truth that I was really truly set free, and that was the first step.

It was so hard to face the accountability that I did what I did. Nobody gave me those pills, nobody encouraged me, that whole plan was all me. I stopped blaming Diamond and my parents. But when my therapist said to me 'it isn't your bullies fault either,' I was enraged. How was none of this Zach's fault. he was the reason behind it all. I'd still be the normal me if Zach hadn't messed up my life. All of this was his fault.

It took me two whole weeks before I finally came to the conclusion she was right, I had to take accountability for my actions. If I ever truly wanted to be happy, I'd have to forget him. Everyday that I was moping around feeling sorry for myself playing the victim, he was winning.

Once I realized that, it started to pick up from there. I excelled through the rest of my therapy because I used my new hate for Zach as fuel. Instead of wanting to get right for me, I was doing it to prove Zach and all those other kids wrong. Let me give you a quick life lesson, don't ever do something out of revenge. Revenge is propped up to be such a great thing, but if you're not actually doing things for the right reasons, it's a giant waste of time. Trust me, I'd know.

I wrote a letter to Zach telling him to come visit me. I rehearsed the whole thing over in my head. He'd walk through the door, see how happy I was, how I wasn't depressed, or anxious, how I was able to just be myself, and he'd see my confidence and instantly apologize. All of them would. They'd all say 'oh my gosh, we were wrong about Alex! He is such a cool guy!' Well, Zach never showed, and I had even reached out to Diamond and she told me that Zach wanted nothing to do with me.

I had just spent four months trying to get better for HIM. I did it for him! Everyday I got up out of that bed, and went down to that therapy room, and poured my guts out! Everyday I did those stupid breathing and meditating exercises! All for what? To just get rejected once again? After all that, I still wasn't good enough? I spiraled really bad after that.

I didn't care. What was the point of getting better if I didn't get to actually feel anything from it? I was in this really dark spot for I don't know how long, and they all tried to help me, but I was a lost cause. Then this new girl came in. Her name was Michelle, and when I saw her, I saw a lot of myself. The tiredness in her eyes, she looked like she was just so done, mentally and physically. Her face was expressionless, she looked like she hadn't felt anything real in years. I got flooded by all these memories. Memories of Zach and Diamond and all of it. I was reliving some of my darkest memories, and they felt so real. I felt just like I was there, except this time, it was ten times worse. All the pain, sorrow, anger, it was amplified. It felt like I was stuck, and I couldn't do anything. No matter what happened, I'd never be able to escape their grasp. I'd always hear their voices in my head. They'd always be there telling me how worthless I was, and discouraging me from ever being happy.

That night I didn't sleep at all. I just laid there for hours going over all the messed up things that happened to me. All the things I wish I could change about my life. All the people I wish I didn't hurt or push away. How different my life would have been if I was just normal. Michelle sparked something in me, I don't know what, but she did something to me. Seeing her all messed up like that, I wanted to help her. No human should feel that way. No person should feel like their life is worthless, or they aren't enough. That's when I made the connection. Michelle was me, and if someone didn't do something to change it, there'd be more of us.

I started taking my therapy seriously. I actually tried to get better, but this time, for me. I did it so that I could be happy, and I could be strong. I needed to do this. It was my mission. I would be the one to instill hope into all these other people who were suffering the same thing as I was; a screwed up society that puts all these pressures on kids to be skinny and be popular. A society where the number of likes and views you get determines if you matter as a person or not. I was a byproduct of a broken system, and I needed to get better so that I could prove, even with the whole world against you, the odds are always in your favor. You can do anything if you really put your mind to it. And yes, I had slip ups and days where I felt bad, but no matter what, I kept getting up and I always stood strong.

Chapter 6
POV Connor

When Alex opened up to me I nearly fell out of the chair. The things he told me, the way he's felt, it made me sick. I'd been called names and been cursed at, but never anything like that. I mean, that sounded horrible. It really puts into perspective how lucky some of us are. I would say my life was a luxurious one compared to Alex. Not that it was a competition on who had it worse, but still. I was so proud of him. Not as my future boyfriend, or at least I hoped him to be, but as a person. To hit rock bottom and manage to come back to the top stronger than before. I don't know many people who could do that.

I learned a lot about Alex, and I felt like things were off to a decent start. I mean, it definitely was not what I was expecting. Who opens up about their darkest memories before the first date? But different was okay. I liked different. I've come to the conclusion that you have to live your life for you and nobody else. Meaning, sometimes in life we forget to do the things that make us happy because we spend all of our time doing what others want.

We stop living our life for us, and instead, start to devote every waking hour to being the person that our parents want us to be. Or a teacher, friend, or partner. It doesn't matter who it is, but we change for them.

Now, I know that nine out of ten guys wouldn't have told me that about themselves. They'd hide it like a bad secret, but Alex was unique. He made this horrible ugly thing and turned it into his strength. He said enough is enough, and he did what I'd been trying to do for years; he started living his life for him. He owned who he was regardless of how it made him stick out, or different it made him. It was like he was this super human who was immune to the conviction of others. It was incredible.

He didn't care that he was this gay guy who defied all the odds and overcame the impossible. I fell in love with him because, after that day, he never let anyone get in the way of happiness, and it worked. You could see it in the way he walked, that he really believed in himself. The way he spoke with such certainty, as if he truly believed what he was saying. He had such a strong, confident personality.

I wanted to spend every waking minute of my

life with him. I wanted to wake up every day to his bright smile. Spend every day listening to him rant for hours and hours talking about all the ways he planned on saving the world. Make giant messes in the kitchen and argue about who was going to clean it up. I was looking forward to Friday nights hanging out building these giant pillow forts in the living room and watching corny rom-coms. I wanted to make him not only my lover, but my best friend. That's how much he meant to me.

I know I only knew him for like three hours, but it was something about him. The energy that radiated off of him, the way his smile made every-thing feel like it was all okay. We wouldn't be the normal couple that had picnic dates and got along, but I didn't care. I knew that a relationship with him would mean doing all sorts of crazy, kooky things I'd never imagined doing. He'd force me to go way out of my comfort zone; I was okay with that though. I was looking forward to being the happiest guy on Earth with him by my side, but first, we'd have to get past our first date.

We made plans for the following Friday to go to this planetarium. Even though I had asked him out, he chose where we went because, to be honest,

I didn't think he'd say yes. I was so taken back that I had the chance to actually go on a date with him that I couldn't even think. I'd never really been on a date before, and to be honest, I wasn't sure if I ever would know what it felt like. I had this whole vision in my head of how it would go, the conversations we'd have, and how the whole night would play out. However, I knew what was in my head and what would actually happen were two different things, and that scared me. I like to know what's going on. I hate going into situations blind. I want to know all the details ahead of time, and in scenarios like this, where it's unpredictable, I tend to get a little crazy. My anxiety kicks in and all I do is fixate on it. I try to keep myself busy and not think about it, but the more I try not to, the more I actually think about it. It's always the small stuff that sends me over the edge. I freak out over not having a cute outfit, or my hair not being perfect, because my stress level is practically maxed.

I must have gone to the mall three times that week and bought four different outfits. I didn't want to wear something too dressy, but also not too casual. I had this button up shirt with jeans, but I looked like I was going to work a meeting.

I bought these nice sweatpants with a hoodie, but when I got home, I looked like I was getting ready to go for a jog. Finally, I settled on these cute ripped jeans I had in my closet and a sweater. It was a tie-dye mix of red, blue and orange.

On Thursday night I barely slept. I was pacing my room for almost four hours before the sun finally rose. I was so nervous, I didn't know what to do or say. Should I get him a gift? Was a rose romantic? Should I get him a stuffed animal? I asked myself what I would want, and it was easy: chocolate. I love chocolate, but all that was so cliche. I wanted to do something unique and original. I wanted to put some thought into it, and have it mean something. So, I went out and bought this cute little black and white heart shaped gift box. The top was white with a black heart print, and the bottom a solid black. Inside, I filled it with white pearls and small gifts. Cinnamon scented mini hand sanitizers, a CD from his favorite album, some cute little heart shaped stickers, a postcard from New York, and a beaded bracelet from this little shop in the mall with hearts on it. I felt confident in it. I knew he would love it.

This whole concept was really new to me. I'd

never cared about someone like this before. With every other guy I'd been with, I didn't really care what happened from it. I never wanted anything from my other relationships like this. I really, really wanted this to work. Alex was the one. You know when you sit down and you think 'what do I want my future husband, (or whoever you plan on marrying), to be like?' You get this whole vision in your head. You have this idea of the life you'll build together. You start to think about all the fun things you can't wait to do with them. The love you'll share for each other, and you have that perfect image all figured out in your head. Alex was all of that for me.

He gave me all this energy to want to do better. I started cooking instead of getting takeout. I was exercising three times a day, and was actually sticking to it. I even found the time to clean out my apartment and donate all my old clothes and stuff. All these things I never had the energy to do, but now all of a sudden, I couldn't keep still. Call it nervous energy or whatever you want, but that week leading up to our date was one of the most productive weeks of my life.

Chapter 7
POV Alex

When I opened up to Connor I was sure he'd run. I wouldn't have blamed him, I sounded like a total mess. When it comes to mental health in society's eyes, you're either crazy or you're not. Once you're branded crazy, you'll forever be crazy. I can't tell you how many times someone got worried I had relapsed all because I had a bad day. Or every time I got agitated and someone around me would remind me of breathing exercises. It's like everyone views you as this ticking time bomb ready to go off. I didn't think Connor would see things the way they actually were.

I thought Connor would be like everyone else and look at me and see this crazy suicidal person, but that wasn't me. Yes, I get mad and sad, and I even yell at times, but I'm a person. I have emotions, but people always think that because I've been through all that crazy stuff and my story is different from others that I'm this emotionally unstable wreck. When in reality, I'm probably the best I've ever been in years.

When I walk into a room with a bunch of strangers they see this guy. They see that he's got good posture and he presents himself well. They see that he's professional, and he seems pretty decent, and then I get to talking. Now, all of a sudden, I'm a gay guy who tried to kill himself because he fell in love with a straight guy. I'm not professional, I'm unstable. My masculinity is challenged because of my sexuality. My credibility is shot, nobody wants to trust a mentally ill person. It's like I'm this whole new person, when in reality, nothing has changed. But somehow, I went from the professional to the basket case that is hopeless.

For a long time, I never really talked about my past because I hated how nobody could ever look past it, but now, I talk about it for that reason because I'm not alone in my fight. So many people out there are going through exactly what I went through, and society has taught us that we shouldn't talk about the bad. We should sweep it under the rug and act like it didn't happen. Well, how do we ever see a change if we continue like that? We see change when we force people to hear us. I share my story so that others can find their strength and share theirs. So that, together, we can do what has to be done to put an end to all this hate.

I didn't expect Connor to see it the way I saw it. I expected him to give me that look you give when you think someone is nuts. You know, the one where you widen your eyes real big and then squint real tight. Where you almost jump back in your seat from disbelief and think to yourself, 'I need to get away from him,' but he didn't.

For the first time in my life someone didn't show me empathy. He didn't try to act like he knew what I went through. He didn't say something corny like, "I'm sorry but you'll get better." He treated me just the same, in fact, he kind of seemed more intrigued. It all felt too good to be true. Like this was a dream, or a sick joke.

And when he asked me to go on a date with him, like a real date, I couldn't talk. I was speechless. I'd known him for three hours, and we'd spent two of those three hours talking about my six months in a mental institution. Clearly, I was hearing things.

"A-a-a-a-a date?" I stuttered.

"Yes, a date," Connor replied.

"I mean, yeah, I'd love to!" I said.

"Awesome. So, uh, what do you want to do?

Cause I didn't think I'd get this far," He questioned.

"Oh, we could go to that new planetarium downtown," I answered.

"Like the fruit bowl place?" he said as seriously as possible.

That's when I knew I'd marry that man. I knew that from that moment on, I wanted to spend every single day of my life at his side. I wanted to paint our first apartment together. I wanted to buy a house, decorate it, and grow a big garden with a giant pool that we could swim in. Our own little paradise; just the two of us. Spending every day going out adventuring the world, trying new foods, buying new clothes. Living the best life. The life we both deserved. I just could not screw up this first date, which was a lot of pressure I put on myself.

Luckily, we were going to a planetarium so there'd be a bit of time during the date where we'd go inside and watch the show. This way it wasn't just us talking the whole night. It gave me less chance of saying something stupid and chasing him away. I just hoped he wouldn't be bored out of his mind, because not many people like astronomy like I do.

I've always loved astronomy and the stars. It's so mesmerizing and beautiful when you think about it. When you see the other planets and the stars. It's almost empowering. If all of that could be created, the stars, the galaxies, and the planets, the limits of what we could do are endless. It's almost like a reality check for that giant enormous task that seems almost impossible. It reminds us that no matter what it is, saving twenty bucks, or buying your first car, it's so minute compared to the billions of stars and infinite universes out there. It's truly incredible and inspiring.

In fact, one of my dream dates had been to go to a planetarium but my ex's found that stuff 'boring and uninteresting.' Although, I can't tell you how many football games I've had to sit through for them. Hours and hours I'd sit in those seats drinking my ten dollar beer that they didn't even have the decency to buy for me, all the while totally unaware what was going on in the game, just sitting there daydreaming and occasionally clapping when everyone else would. However, none of that mattered. What mattered was that Connor was taking me, and I was going to have fun. Even if he thought we were going to get fruit bowls.

That whole week, all I could think about was him. Should I text him or would that be too clingy? But what if he thinks I'm not interested? Should I buy him a gift? What would I get him? Chocolate? No! The dude is like a total gym buff, no way he eats that stuff. Ugh, decisions. I'm horrible at those. After several hours of looking up cute ideas online, I finally found this cute key-chain I knew he'd love.

Thursday night I was such a wreck I nearly passed out. I couldn't eat or sleep, or even think. I was so worried and afraid of messing things up. Connor was probably in bed sleeping while I was up all night worrying. To him, this was probably nothing, but to me, it was everything.

I've always had one rule that I think has been beneficial to my recovery, and that's to never let my happiness depend on another person. Being with Connor was violating that, big time. It was a gamble going on that date. Except, instead of fifty dollars at stake, it was my mental health. Connor reminded me a lot of Zach, and I know how twisted that sounds, but it's the truth. I'd been with several guys in my life, but there were only two that I loved. They were Zach and Connor. The difference was that Connor wouldn't treat me like Zach. Or at least I hoped.

That's when I started to freak out. What if Connor was just another Zach? I felt like this with Zach, and Diamond warned me. You know what I told her? "Don't be silly, that'll never happen," and I was wrong, and it cost me everything. What if I was wrong again? What if I opened up and risked it all to just get screwed over again. What if Connor was just another manipulative guy who planned on using me?

I started driving myself crazy because I hated Zach. I hated how he had this grasp on my life. How, because of one person, ONE person out of the seven billion people on this earth, my trust in others had been destroyed. I hated how I could never just be happy anymore. Every time a good thing came my way, all I could think about was 'man this is gonna hurt when it's gone.' So, I decided I wasn't going with Connor. I wasn't ready. I had to cancel.

I didn't want to, but what choice did I have? All

I could think about was him leaving me and how it would hurt. How I'd be so dependent on him for love and affection, that when he walked away, I'd be crippled. Because that's what I do. I love hard. I give it my all, even when I know I shouldn't. Connor would ruin me.

Chapter 8
POV Connor

I pulled up to the address he gave me and I waited in the parking lot for about an hour and fifteen minutes, and nothing. I got stood up. I thought I did right by telling the truth. I really did, but I was wrong. I was also stupid. Stupid to believe that someone like Alex, someone so perfect, would like me. I mean, I should have seen it coming.

In my life, things never go right. Everything I do starts off all flowery and colorful, but then boom, it turns into a big fiery explosion. It's okay, Alex wasn't the first person to walk out of my life, and I was sure he wouldn't be the last. No, unfortunately Alex was just one of many names on the long list of people who walked out of my life.

You'd think that after all those times it would get easier, but it doesn't.

The first person to walk out of my life was Chase. We met in the first grade. He sat next to me and we were counting buddies. We hated each other, he was the most annoying kid I'd ever met. He would always move my arm while I was coloring to make me slip up and go outside the lines. When lunch came, he'd always cut me in line so that he could go first and get the best snacks before they ran out. I did not like him, and it stood like that until fifth grade.

Mrs. Fisher was this little old lady who had been teaching for years. Her teaching style was very old fashioned. For example, she would always pair you together with someone you didn't get along with. Her reasoning was so that it would force you to make new friends. Hence how me and Chase went from hating each other to actually being friends.

We got paired up to do this science project on the biomes. We had to make a giant poster talking about the ecosystem and the food chain, all this science stuff that bored me to death. Even though we were in groups, we did our own projects because he and I still couldn't see eye to eye. He wanted to print the pictures out from the computer and I wanted to draw them. He wanted to pick Antarctica and I wanted to do the rain forest. So, we decided we'd do our own projects. When it came time towards the end when it was due, we agreed to go to his house and decide which one was the best, and that would be the one we would turn in.

It was the only way we'd get anything done because he was so controlling. He wanted everything his way, and God forbid you suggest a new idea to him, he'd lose it. Seven times he went to Mrs. Fisher asking if he could swap partners, but Mrs. Fisher was a tough old lady and she wasn't going to cave into Chase.

Three weeks I spent doing my part of the project, and from what I saw, his was looking like a total disaster. Now, mine wasn't no Mona Lisa, but at least it looked neat and organized. His poster board was all ripped and wrinkled. The corners creased, and the printed pictures in black and white. He used so much glue that the purple from the glue stick had bled through and you couldn't even tell what you were looking at. Yet, he still kept going. I offered to let him help me but he wanted it his way.

When the time finally came to choose between the two, I knew how it would go down. I told my mom to stick in the neighborhood because I didn't plan on staying any longer than five minutes. I'd show him mine, offer to put his name on it, and then I'd leave. I had no intentions of staying any longer than I absolutely had to. After all, I really, really disliked him. He was like a total control freak, and nasty. What idiot would possibly want to be friends with him?

Well, I soon found out that I was the idiot. I walked from my car and rang his doorbell. He answered it and my mom drove off. We didn't talk at all. We just walked through his kitchen and down into the basement where he had everything set up. He had a nice house, and his mom seemed nice. She offered me a juice box, and made me feel really welcomed. She was nothing like him.

When we went into his basement, he had a big flat screen TV with a gaming console and computer. He had a little table set up where he had his 'project.' I was impressed with how neat everything was. this was totally not what I would have expected for him. He seemed too sloppy to have a nice, neat, hang out like that. The mini fridge had juice boxes and water, all neatly placed on the shelves in three straight rows. On the table next to it, this little box filled with snacks, and on the floor next to that, a small little garbage pail.

I was getting mad at myself because I didn't want to admit it, but I began to realize I was wrong about Chase. Then finally, I couldn't control it. "Is that the new X invaders?" I blurted out. That game was sold out everywhere! I'd been trying to get a copy for like two months, but everywhere I went was out of stock. How'd he manage to get it?

"I slept out front of the store on opening night," Chase said.

"Can we play?" I asked.

Just like that, the friendship had started. From that day on, Chase and I became best friends. I learned a lot about him. He wasn't actually as bad as I thought he was. I mean, don't get me wrong, he was still annoying at times, and a bit controlling, but hey, we all have our own quirks. Behind those quirks was an amazing personality with a great sense of humor. He had a very original sense of humor, that very unique one in a million type of humor. There was never a dull moment during the entire time of our friendship. We were practically inseparable. Then, sophomore year came.

At that point, we were at the peak of our friendship. We'd been best friends for almost five years, and had some of the best memories to come from it. He was one of the only people that I trusted and could count on. However, that was also the same summer I came out as gay, and I was worried about telling him. I didn't have a problem telling my other friends because they were girls, and well, quite frankly, girls don't care about that stuff. It was one less guy they had to worry about catcalling them when they walked by.

Guys, however, are the total opposite. I find that really funny and ironic. Straight guys are so afraid of unwanted sexual advances from a gay guy, but than turn around and treat woman the exact same way, if not worse. The difference, however, is that when they do it, the girl is 'asking for it,' or 'it's not wrong.' However, when a straight guy texts us first, makes all the first moves, practically pushing them-self onto us, we're still in the wrong because we were the 'pushy' ones. Everyone believes the typical stereotype and doesn't even bother to question if the gay kid was right, they just assume, and most of the time they are wrong. They call us all kinds of slurs and curse us out for no other reason than because we had the audacity to look at them, because, god forbid, their masculinity gets threatened. Don't get me wrong, there are probably some gay guys out there who are pesky, pushy, and pry, but, for the most part, we're all respectful. I guess I was just worried that Chase would be one of those uneducated guys who doesn't know anything about the LGBTQ+ community, and that he would base his entire thought process on stereotypes.

To my surprise, he wasn't. He congratulated me and was supportive. That was not something I was expecting. I mean, some things were weird, like when he'd see a cute girl, there'd be that tiny bit of awkward tension, and vice versa for me when a guy would come over and talk to us. It was all new though, and I expected these things to happen. My whole life, everyone assumed I was straight. They never guessed or thought about me being gay, and now, here I was. I knew it would take some getting used to. I was just happy that it didn't blow up in my face because I really liked Chase, he was funny and always knew how to make me laugh. I relied on him for a lot of things, like making me laugh when I was feeling down, and just being an all around good friend, and that's important. We all need someone in our lives to listen to us when we need to vent, or to cheer us up and make us feel better about ourselves. Chase didn't really change much, and that was just all the more proof of what a good friend he truly was.

Before I knew it, things went back to normal. We still hung out all the time, and we texted each other a lot, but I had one problem, and that was I didn't want things to go back to normal. I was different, and that meant that my new normal was different. If I was being completely honest, I didn't like video games, and I didn't like talking about sports. I liked clothes and fashion. I wanted to step back from my masculine side and let my feminine side come out. Now, this is where all the problems come into play because Chase wasn't like that, and how do two polar opposites stay friends? How do two people who now have totally different interests and hobby's make conversation and hang out?

It's kind of impossible, but I had this feeling that me and him would make it work. Turns out I was wrong.

As I slowly developed into the newer version of myself I could see subtle things changing in our friendship. Little comments here and there that I chose to ignore and overlook, but it felt like Chase wasn't the same anymore. Whenever we'd go out there'd be really awkward moments of silence, where I'd feel myself being judged. Than one day I finally confronted him about it. I asked him why he was acting the way he was. I wasn't trying to be confrontational, I just wanted to know why all of a sudden there was this drastic change in the way he treated me. At first he denied it, but I knew him better than that, I knew there was something he wasn't telling me. So I asked him again, this time he paused for a moment before freaking out on me saying that he was okay with me being gay but that didn't mean that he would support me being a 'stupid tranny.' He even continued on to say that god made me a guy and I shouldn't try and change that.

When he said those things I was hurt. I didn't know what to say because I never thought my best friend would think of me in such a hurtful way. That in itself was enough to make me cry. Firstly, I was not transgender, and for him to just be ignorant and assume that was frustrating. Secondly, if I was to be trans, just to know that's how he would view me it really broke me. I could think of worse things for me to do than paint my nails and wear a cropped shirt. Why did this have to matter? Why does the clothes I wear, or the style I chose determine whether or not someone can be friends with me or not?

I was so astonished with what he had said that I just stood there in silence before he walked away, and that was the last I ever saw him. I tried calling and texting, but I never got a response. That seems pretty short and anti-climatic for the end of an almost five year friendship, but that's how it went down. No explanation after that, nothing. We just separated, and he went on like I never existed.

If I'm being honest, that hurt more than anything because I did nothing wrong. I was just being myself. If I did something wrong, like I slept with his ex or I lied to him, maybe I could see him doing something like that, but just calling it quits because I wanted to be happy? Thinking back on it that night, I got even more mad because he was the one who walked away, and it should have been me. I should have been the one to get angry and storm off, and he should have been the one standing there dumbfounded and confused, rather than me. Yet, there I was, totally blindsided by all of it, standing there all alone watching him walk away, but that's kind of how my life goes. I always want to believe the best in everyone, and majority of the time, I get let down.

The sad thing is that Chase wasn't the only one to just up and leave. After Chase, it was Rachel. I met Rachel in sixth grade. She was an eighth grader, and was my assigned escort for my first day of middle school. It was weird, because normally, the older kids are supposed to hate the little kids, but Rachel was really nice. She walked me all around the school introducing me to her favorite teachers. When I met with my friends at lunch, they all talked about how their guides were rude and impatient, but Rachel was not like that at all. In fact, I thought Rachel and I were friends. Even though she had three years on me, it didn't matter.

We seemed to hit it off. I think a big part of it was that I was much more mature than the other kids my age. Most preteens are immature, they laugh at fart jokes, and they have no idea when to stop messing around. I was different. I was the kid who was quiet, did what he was told, and always got good grades. Now, by no means was I Mr. serious, but I knew that there was a time and place for it. So, even though Rachel was older than me, our mindsets were a lot alike.

After my first day, I thought I'd never see Rachel again. However, everyday after that, she'd come find me in the cafeteria and we'd go outside and eat our lunch together. I didn't mind, and soon I invited Chase to join us. The three of us were an iconic trio. Rachel was the dumb crazy party animal. She knew how to make everyone laugh, whether it be making a stupid face or telling a corny joke. She was always smiling and goofing around. Chase was the brave one. There wasn't anything he wasn't scared to do. He was unpredictable, and spontaneous. Then you had me, the smart one. I was the one who kept everyone from getting in trouble.

Rachel was the first one I came out to. She was a junior and I was a freshman. She didn't care at all. In fact, she helped me come out to Chase before that all went down the drain. When that did happen, it took everything in me to stop her from exploding on him. She was more hurt than I was. Rachel really cared about me, and to see how Chase did what he did, it hurt her. It hurt her because I was a part of her, and to this day, I don't know how she turned on me the way she did. How she went from almost beating up Chase to ghosting me and acting like I didn't even exist.

I know the reason, though. She may not have ever told me, but I know why she did what she did. I wasn't cool enough. I could tell that's what it was. Slowly, she started to distance herself from me. We maybe saw each other once or twice a week. In school, she always had a project at lunch, or some stupid excuse as to why she couldn't sit with me. What she didn't know was that I saw through her lies. I knew that she didn't have a project, because I caught her more than once. She said she was in the science lab making up a test, but was actually flirting with James.

She also didn't know that I followed James on social media So, every time she lied saying she was at work or had an overload of homework, I was watching as James posted her with all their new friends having the time of their lives. I don't know what hurt more, the fact that she was lying to me, or that she seemed so happy and I wasn't there. I'd never seen her smile like that with me. In fact, I'd never even seen that side of her before. I mean, she was happy and all, but this, this was a different type of happiness. This time she was really happy, as if all those years of smiles and laughs she was just faking.

As time went on, I watched as my best friend turned into a complete stranger in a matter of two months. We never talked it out, we never even addressed it. It didn't take a rocket scientist to figure it out. She was one of the popular kids now. She got invited to the parties, and started smoking. Gradually, she didn't find anything fun anymore. She felt the adrenaline rush of driving down a highway, in a sports car with a bunch of hot guys, and now, all of a sudden, she didn't want to go back to her old boring life.

Sitting outside, eating a peanut butter sandwich with me was considered lame, when she could be making out James in the school bathroom. Playing board games with me on a Friday night sounded stupid, when she could be out getting drunk and having the best time of her life. I mean, the choice was simple, at least for her it was.

So, we both just walked away from the friendship. We never argued, or even talked about it, we just stopped talking. No explanation, no nothing. That's how it had to be, because I think deep down, we both cared about each other too much. But, neither one of us wanted to change our lives. I know that if I decided to start smoking and partying, and I became this intense rager, she'd have welcomed me with open arms, but that isn't me. So, just like that, another person walked out on me.

I'd lost tons of people in my life, more than I could even count. You know how many people that I was friendly with that just stopped talking to me when I came out? Chase and Rachel were just two of the most important people in my life, and now, just like them, Alex would do the same thing. So, filled with anger and rage, I started my car, getting ready to drive off and go home all alone. I went to look behind as I shifted the gear from park to drive, and there he was. Standing behind my car from my rear-view mirror I saw him standing there with that hopeful twinkle in his eyes, the one I'd fallen in love with.

Chapter 9
POV Alex

If you're someone like me, someone who falls really hard and loves with everything they've got, love can ruin you. Love can make you do things you'd never even think of doing. It changes you into this self destructive monster who'd hurt anyone or anything just to make that one special person happy. You'll lie, hurt, attack, and lash out at everyone but the one person who deserves it the most. The worst part about it is, you don't even realize what's going on. You're blinded by it, and when they leave, because they will leave, it hurts a lot; like a band aid being ripped off a cut. You feel this pain, and you look back at your path, and you see all the destruction you'd done, like a tornado passing through a town. You can't fix it, so there you are, stuck all alone because you pushed everyone away believing that the person you loved would never leave your side, but they did. And, all those people you called crazy and delusional? Well, they were right. That's the love I knew.

On the flip side of that, love can be the most beautiful thing in the world. Look at a baby, that's a product of love. Look back to 9/11, how all those people ran into the rubble to save lives. I'm not just talking about first responders, I'm talking about random people who knew not one single thing about search and rescue. People who could've ran but decided to stay and help, all out of love. Think about the thousands of doctors and nurses who got up everyday during the Corona virus pandemic and risked their lives to save other people. They did it for no other reason than love. The selfless men and women who fight on the front lines in foreign countries for our freedom. It's all out of love. There may be a lot of hate in this world, but let me tell you something, love will always win.

I may have had one bad experience with love, but I wouldn't let it define my entire future. I wasn't about to let Zach determine my happiness for the rest of my life, so, I got in my car and I left. I was going on that date, no matter how scared I was. Sometimes we need to stop thinking and just do it. We need to just put ourselves on auto pilot and go with our gut. Being with Connor felt right.

I felt safe when I thought of him. I felt like he was my home.

When I got there, I was afraid he would have left already, but his car was still in the parking lot. I parked my car and started to walk over to him. I could see his reflection in the mirror of his car; he looked angry. I screwed it up. I knew it. I went to turn around, what was the point of going over there? He'd just get even more mad and yell at me. But I had to. I owed him an explanation. I needed him to know it wasn't him, and it was me. I didn't want him to spend the next two weeks thinking, 'what did I do wrong?' When in fact, he was perfect.

I took a deep inhale as I got close, preparing for him to lose his temper and go off. It's what I'd do if I got stood up, but I guess he saw me coming up because he got out of his car. This was the part where he'd make a big scene and the cops would get called. The part where I'd run to my car crying because, once again, I screwed up. I knew all too well how these things worked, and when he started running at me I froze. I froze because I didn't know whether to run, or call for help, or what. But, instead of a fist, I was greeted with this humongous hug. He wrapped both his arms around me and squeezed super tight. I just stood there with my arms at my side, in shock. He took this deep breath in and rested his head on my shoulder. I don't think I'd ever felt more safe in my life. Even though we were in the middle of a parking lot in probably one of the worst towns in the county, I'd never felt like that before. For the first time in my life, I put down all my walls, and the two of us stood there for five minutes, arms wrapped around each other.

By the time we'd finally let go and decided to go in, our show was already half way through, so we decided to go to the beach. It was evening, and the sky was starting to get dark, probably like seven o'clock. I remember getting in his car and thinking it had to be a joke. I was dreaming or something. There was no way that I could possibly be that lucky, but there he was, sitting next to me driving the car, taking me to what would eventually become the best night of my life.

It was a very awkward beginning. I didn't know what to say, or even if I should say anything. He barely talked, so I decided I'd turn on the radio.

We were on the bridge heading into the downtown area where all the rides and the beaches were. I remember looking down at the water and all the boats. The sun was setting, so everything was orange and yellow. The radio was on, and I went to change it but he stopped me. "No, don't change it, I love this song!" he said as he turned up the volume a little bit. He started to hum along to the beginning, and subconsciously, I started to as well. I'd never even heard the song before but, somehow, I instinctively knew the lyrics. Right before the chorus came on, he reached over, blasting the volume all the way and rolled down the windows. We sat there singing along together, the both of us in unison. The wind was blasting me in the face ruining my hair, but I didn't care. It was one of those times where we were both so into the moment neither of us cared. We didn't care that we both sounded like dying cows, or that the cars next to us probably thought we were nuts. We were so stuck in the moment, the both of us wanting it to stay like that forever. It's one of those things that I look back to now when I'm having a bad day and smile.

I'd never been happier in my life. The rest of

the night I was on cloud nine. We parked the car a little ways off and walked down the pier as all the seagulls squawked and flew over our heads. We did a couple of the games at the arcade, but you know how that goes. You spend ten dollars on tokens and get enough tickets for a small package of candy. What's even more funny is that you actually think you won something. From there, we went to the claw machine, and we won this little stuffed octopus. Most couples go with teddy bears, but we weren't most couples.

I won him a little monkey from the darts game. I was five points away from getting the giant one but, of course, I missed my shot. I'm convinced those games are rigged so that you never win. Either way, Connor was happy. It didn't matter what I got him, as long as it came from me. He really loved me, and this was new to me. I knew what it felt like to love someone, but never to be loved back. It was kind of weird, especially when you're not used to it. You have someone just being nice to you all the time. Looking at you out of the corner of their eye and smiling, admiring you like a piece of art. Holding hands, walking together, it was amazing.

Finally, at the end of the night, we found ourselves at the beach. We were sitting there in complete silence. The only sound was the waves crashing on the shore. I turned to start talking to him, and as soon as I did, he kissed me. I wasn't expecting it, and at first I was surprised, but it was one of those good surprises. Like a 'I can't believe this is happening right now' surprise. A surprise where you want to jump up and down and scream on the top of your lungs.

That was my first time ever actually physically feeling love. I could feel how connected we were in those few moments. I could feel the intensity of his feelings for me emitting off of him like heat. I, never in a million years, would have thought someone would feel that way about me. In those moments, I forgot all about my past. I had completely let go, like letting go of a balloon in a big open field.

"I take it you really like me?" I said.

He looked me dead in the eye so I could tell he wasn't lying.

"Yes," he said very softly, but at the same time, with such passion.

"How about you? Do you feel the same?" he

said to me as he gently caressed my cheek with his hand.

I took a second to really think about my answer. If I said yes, that would mean going all in. That would mean I couldn't decide I wanted to bail on him anymore, it was all or nothing.

And of course I said, "Yes. Yes I do."

Chapter 10
POV Connor

Two very important things happened that night. The first being Alex and I had our first kiss. The second being we also made it official. We were finally boyfriend and boyfriend, which felt really weird to say out loud. I've always been insecure about my sexuality, and it took me two years just to be able to say the words 'I'm gay.' I remember the first time I got my nails done. I'd seen these really cute purple acrylics online and I wanted them so bad. I screenshotted the picture and I'd look at it every night before I went to bed. I'd lay there thinking about how they'd feel on my fingers. How, when the time came that I could get them,

I'd be so extra with it. Then, came the pain. The pain of knowing that I had to wake up everyday and pretend to be something I wasn't.

My family supported me. Well, in their eyes they did. If you ask them, they'd portray me as this ungrateful brat who was always pushing his luck. The thing is, my parents didn't care I was gay, as long as I acted straight. They'd say things like, "oh we love you," and then say stuff like "ew that's just disgusting, why don't you act like a man." That's the crazy thing about homophobia; it can be anyone.

When most people hear the word 'homophobia,' they think about some crazy radical extremist, almost like a terrorist. Someone who's main goal is to kill all the gay people, but what if I told you that was a total misconception? What if I told you that the sweet old lady at church who gives out the Holy Communion every Sunday was teaching hate to her sophomore religion class? You'd think it would be a lie, but it's not.

Her name was Mrs. Robins. She came off as the nicest person you'd ever meet. She was the 'mom' of the school. If you weren't feeling good, she'd write you a note so you could stay back from your next class. She always had snacks, and would pay for your lunch if you didn't have the money. She was also very religious, hence why she taught religion class. She never missed mass, not once. Every Sunday she was at church, and during the week, she said her rosaries twice daily. She'd read a verse of the bible every morning and night, and the first thirty minutes of class, we'd all pray together. So, think about it, at eight periods a day, that's four hours a day praying.

At first, she had me fooled. She would say stuff like "God loves everyone," "God created all of us equal and in his own image," all she talked about was how she enjoyed helping others. She really had me fooled at first, than one day the real side of her came out.

We walked into class, and she had this very serious look, which was odd for her. Normally, she would smile and tell us all a joke as we came in, but that day she didn't. We sat down in our seats, we all could sense something was up. She was just sitting at her desk, very serious. The bell rang and she still sat there. Finally, she spoke.

"Class," she began.

"Today's conversation is going to be a very

controversial one. I don't want to step on any toes, or offend anyone. But, I want to talk about homosexuality," she paused.

I sat straight up in the chair. I got really tense and felt like I was burning up. My palms were clammy, and I felt like everyone was staring at me.

"If you think you'll be offended, you are more than welcome to leave, no judgement," she spoke.

Now, I could've gotten up and walked out, but in what position would that put me in? I wasn't completely out yet, not to the majority of the people, so I sat there.

"Okay. So, before I actually start talking, I want to let everyone know that I love and support gay people," she said, and for a second, I felt a burst of happiness.

"I just think that the fact that they are allowed to get legally married is a total disgust, and disrespect of my religion. " she continued.

My happiness quickly turned into anger. That anger, into pain and sadness.

"If you look in the bible, it will tell you that marriage is a scriptural term. And, as a Catholic, I denounce gay marriage because it is a sin. It goes against the guidelines of what a marriage should be. In the bible it says a marriage should be fruit-ful, and two men or two women can't be fruitful. When a gay couple gets together, it should be called a civil union," she said.

I could continue on with her lecture, but I think you get the point.

The reason I am bringing all this up is that it's not just the nut job who has a confederate flag and Assault Rifle that we have to worry about. It can be anyone. Our world is filled with hate and inequality, and we're all too blind to even see it. I guess I was just worried because I hadn't the slight-est idea of what dating Alex was going to bring. I never had anyone that I could really talk to or ask advice, besides a bunch of straight people who had no idea what it meant to be gay.

Think about it. How can a gay son go over to his father and say, "Dad, my husband is mad at me. What do I do?" Now, if he was straight, the father could give him all this advice from personal experience, but he isn't. It's not like with straight couples where the road is all paved and you can talk to just about anyone and they'll tell you some decent advice. I don't mean to sound stuck up, but if you're not gay, you wouldn't understand our problems. It's just the truth. I had someone tell me once, "just come out, it can't be that hard." As if this person had any clue what I was going through. I blame it all on a lack of education and ignorance.

Our schools are extremely biased. They teach sex education and talk all about straight people problems. They mention the word 'homosexual' once, and then you never see it again. Up until I was about seventeen, I had no idea the difference between a non-binary and a binary person. I didn't know what a cisgendered person was, or what pan-sexual meant. You know what I did know? I knew how to label a diagram of the female reproductive system. Anything I know related to LGBTQ+ I found out through the internet.

I guess that's why I want to change the world. We live in a flawed society and not nearly enough people are talking about it. What we need to do is bring to light the thousands of people who would rather end their lives than have to live in such a ruthless world in which they have to suppress who they are. All the kids who go to school everyday just to be met by bullying and hate. Those same kids who have to then go home to families who openly criticize and hate on them.

I'm bringing all this up because we live in a world with some mean, cruel people in it. A world where you can't be gay in public without having to look over your shoulder and worry about if someone is going to say something to you. I'd known that reality all too well, and because of that, I never thought I would be able to say the words 'my boyfriend' out loud. It's still something I have to struggle with. It's not like you come out, and suddenly, all your problems go away. No. They follow you the rest of your life, and that was a lesson I was about to learn.

It was Alex and I's fifth date. We'd done some mostly small stuff, like walks in the park, or swimming in his pool at his apartment complex. So, we decided we'd meet up for coffee at this little shop down the street from the shopping center where he worked. He was on his lunch break, so when I got there, he had already gotten a table and started drinking. It was busy, so I was glad he even managed to get a spot. He got iced coffee with avocado toast because he hadn't eaten yet, and I had this weird berry tea, because personally, I find coffee repulsive.

We were talking about his day, and how he had

this old man come in and yell that they didn't have his size jeans. You know, the typical complaints that all retail workers have to put up with. Anyways, the waitress came over with my order. Alex and I talked, and before we knew it, he needed to get back to work. So, the waitress came back with the check and it said:

"To the two faggots at table 2."

They tell you that to be safe, you shouldn't confront the person, because they might turn violent. Which I'd done my whole life. People would call me names like that, and I'd blow it off, walk away, and act like it didn't happen. You can only do that so many times before you've had enough and you can't bite your tongue anymore, so you explode. That's where they get you. They provoke you, but because you acted first, they spin the whole situation around saying you started it, and all these other lies. I've been in this situation many times, especially in school. Guys would murmur stuff under their breath, and when I confronted them, I'd get in trouble because the teachers only saw or heard me. It didn't matter that I had every right to be mad, I was still seen as the problem, and I was really tired of it.

I stood up on that table, in front of all those people, and I said, "So according to the waitress over there, me and my boyfriend are faggots! So, I'd like to ask if anyone else agrees with her?"

There was a dead silence, like everyone was in a total shock.

"How about you?" I asked the group of women who had been giving us dirty looks the whole time.

"Don't act like I didn't see you giving us looks the whole time! The one in the middle. Yeah, you. Every time we laughed, you'd lean over to your friend and whisper in her ear. I haven't overcome all the troubles of growing up in a school where I was bullied and picked on everyday just to get called a slur by some ignorant waitress. I didn't spend my whole life fighting to be equal like everyone else just to be knocked down again!" I shouted.

I wanted to say more, but the manager had come over and asked me to step down. I didn't fight or resist at all. I stepped down, and he walked us both out, assuring us that he'd speak with the waitress and reprimand her. He even tried to make the order on the house, but I insisted he take my money. I even gave the waitress a five dollar tip. I was fed up with people hating on me for just wanting to be happy. I was so happy with myself, for actually being brave and standing up for once. I just hoped that Alex felt the same way I did.

Chapter 11
POV Alex

Connor and I really seemed to hit off after our first kiss. In a way, it bonded us. The spark I felt, and I'm assuming he did too, was unlike anything I'd ever felt before. I guess after feeling that, I knew I could trust him, and vice versa because we both really opened up to each other. We'd gone on four dates after that, all within three weeks. The pool in my apartment complex, a picnic/walk in the park, we flew kites on the beach, and we went out to some burger place that had a five pound burger, to see who could eat the most of it. Then came the fifth date, which I think really was a turning point.

I was working when I got a text from Connor saying he wanted to meet me on my break. We decided on the coffee shop closest to my job so that I could get back in time. I remember it being the worst day ever. I had a little girl accidentally knock over a display table. Thank god she didn't get hurt, but it all could have been avoided if her mother was paying attention. After that, I had some lady argue with me for fifteen minutes about a return item that she'd clearly worn already. To top all that off, some old man came in with a chip on his shoulder yelling at me because we didn't have jeans in his size. All I could think about was seeing Connor, and his smile.

We got to the coffee shop, and within minutes, I'd forgotten all about those annoying people. He just always knew how to make me laugh. He told me this hilarious story of how on the way there, some couple had broken up in front of him, and the girl got out of the car and was laying on the hood stopping all the traffic. He was the best story teller because he was so dramatic and he'd give the best impersonations of the people. He was always so joyful, I'd never seen him mad before, but that was about to change.

We had this horrible waitress who smelt like body odor and could not make a coffee to save her life. I don't know who hired her, but she must have had some sort of connection because, I know for a fact, she'd never even have passed the interview the way she looked. Her hair all matted together like it hadn't been combed in weeks. The fact that she was allowed to go to work like that amazed me, but Connor had a great way of distracting me from all this.

He started to tell me this story of how he went to an amusement park and rode the big crazy ride that drops you straight down. He promised that we'd take our first vacation to Florida because he had family down there that knew about a bunch of cool places we could go and visit. He had the whole week planned out. He told me he wrote an itinerary, and I thought he was joking, but he actually did. He said we could go in October because the weather would be nice and they'll have the Halloween events going on at all the theme parks. The fact that he was thinking long term meant he really wanted a future. After that, he rambled on for about ten more minutes while I zoned out and started to think about how blessed I really was to have him in my life. It still was so unreal that I could have everything I'd ever dreamed of. It just felt like it was too good to be true.

Before I knew it, time was up, and I had to leave. So, I asked for the check, and when we got the receipt, this amazing waitress we had decided she'd leave us a friendly note on there. Well, Connor lost it. I saw him read it and get that look in his eyes, and I went to stop him, but it was too late. She poked the bear, and she was going to pay the consequences. He ripped her apart in front of everyone, even called out a few other people while he was at it, and just like that, I feel even more in love with him.

When I first came out, my mom was devastated. I mean, she literally cried. After the initial shock wore off, she then did everything in her power to convince me I was wrong. "How do you know you don't like girls if you've never tried? You're just desperate for a relationship and are settling for a guy because you don't think you can get any better. You're wrong, I'm telling you." After all those failed attempts, we finally came to a 'don't ask, don't tell situation.'

She still silently judged me with glares and back sided compliments. She even tried to apologize saying, "I'm sorry I over reacted at first, but it's just that having a gay son is the worst thing a parent can hear, and as much as I want to change you, I can't, so I guess I'll have to deal with it and accept it."

In her eyes, that was a heartfelt apology. I didn't get annoyed though, and for the most part, I was able to hold my tongue. The only time I ever got mad was when she had the nerve to go and say that she was the most supportive parent she knew. At first, I laughed, because I thought it was sarcasm, but when I found out she was telling the truth, or what she thought was the truth, I nearly lost my temper. We got into this big fight that ended with us agreeing to never talk about it again, and we didn't. Not for a long time.

My dad, on the other hand, didn't hide anything. I was called a disappointment everyday of my life for about two months straight. Every time he'd get mad he'd say, "you're a little faggot," or he'd use some other choice words. It came to a point where I couldn't wait to leave my house and never look back. That's all I thought about, was freedom and being able to be who I wanted to be without anyone hating me.

When things got bad with Zach, and my home life was a wreck, I didn't have anywhere to go without being attacked for who I was, and I started to slip and spiral down. I thought about getting help, but where would I go? I didn't drive, or I'd go and visit a support group. I was stuck. I remember sitting down with my mom the night before I tried to take my life the first time, this was before Diamond had found me. We sat down and I tried to explain that her 'supportiveness' was actually hurting me. She, however, took this as me calling her a bad parent and sent me to my room. That night, I locked myself in my room for three hours, and nobody came to check up on me. I'd never felt so alone in my life. I desperately wanted to end it all, but I couldn't. As badly as I wanted to give up, I had this tiny little bit of hope inside of me. This hope that, one day, I'd be able to stand up for myself, and not be forced to take other people's hate.

Connor sticking up for, not just himself, but me too, was brave. Braver than anything I've ever seen. When you're in that situation, it's a tough call to make. When someone is attacking you, and you can hear the hate in their voice and can sense the anger and disgust in them, it's like a hot knife to the heart. For Connor to say and do what he did so quickly and on the spot, was brave.

He didn't need to think about it, he just stood up and said what had to be said. Even though he was probably hurt and in pain, he didn't let that get in the way of speaking his mind, and that was quite possibly the most courageous thing I'd ever seen anyone do.

When I was put into the facility, I wasn't allowed to see any family until I passed a set benchmark. After I reached that criteria, they would finally allow my first visit with my parents. I didn't expect them to show up, if I'm being honest. I thought they hated me. My father thought I was a disappointment before all this. I could only imagine what he would have to say now. I wondered if he lied and told all the family that I was sick, or that I went away on vacation. I couldn't picture him telling everybody the truth. He idolized his image too much to tell anyone his son was in a mental facility.

If they showed up, it would have to be in my therapist's office with her supervising, just in case things got ugly. I walked down the hall with all the doors shut as everyone else met with their parents, and I saw my office all the way at the end of the hall, the only one with the door not shut. Even though I despised my parents, it hurt me to know that they didn't care about me. Your parents made you, they're the reason you're here, so naturally, they should be the ones you could count on the most. The ones who love you the most. Friends come and go, and so do cousins and aunts and uncles, but your parents should never leave your side. Sad truth is that far too many people know this not to be true, and I was about to be one of them.

I had to know for sure, I couldn't just give up on that. Maybe by some grace they were in traffic or something. So, I went over to the door and, to my surprise, both of them were there. They both greeted me with such love and affection. My dad showed more interest in me that day than he did my entire life. My mom handed me a bundle of letters from all my family sending their love and asking how I was. They really had me convinced that they had changed.

Every Wednesday, Friday and Sunday, they showed up at five o'clock for those therapy sessions. My mom would bring this little pink notebook she had and would write down all the little tips and advice my therapist gave her for when I would go back home. Things like, "be attentive," or "listen to what he's actually saying." I really thought they were trying to work on getting better.

When I got home, my bed was all made, and

everything was perfect. Not a speck of dust. Everything was the way I left it. The pillows fixed just right, and my favorite hoodie folded neatly on the bed. It had that clean smell so I could tell it had just been washed. Those first two weeks were like heaven. We all got along like a normal family. Dinner at the table every night at six o'clock. Casual conversations that didn't lead to major arguments. Things that I wasn't used to before, but I liked this new lifestyle.

However, life soon got in the way. My mom would have to work over time, and my dad would be too lazy to cook. So, the nice home cooked meals turned into pizza and burgers. We went from eating together, to scattered all throughout the house, and just like that, everything had reset to the way it was before. My dad started yelling at me for the smallest things. My mom started nit picking on me for everything I did wrong. That little pink notebook soon turned into a dust collector that would get lost in the junk drawer.

When the time came for me to go back to school after rehab, I was a wreck, like beyond scared. I didn't want to face Zach, or any of those kids. I feared it would regurgitate too many ugly feelings.

Over the time I was there, I had managed to forget them, and sort of halfway recuperated from the traumas they put me through. There's so many things that happened in the dark nobody knew about. I was almost on an 'okay' path, but I knew if I went back, I would have surely self-destructed. There was no way I could have dealt with the pain and abuse. Being attacked and targeted everyday, I don't think anyone could deal with that. I begged my parents to let me drop out of school, pleaded with them. My dad, he didn't care. He told me, "it's up to your mother." My mother's response, "I won't let you become some drop out loser and work at a gas station your whole life."

That little note she wrote down, "be attentive," she had forgotten all about that. She didn't hear a word I was saying. All she heard was that her son wanted to drop out of school. I understand where she was coming from, most people with kids would have said the same thing. However, I am not most kids. I had legit reasons on why I wanted to do this. This wasn't about my hate for math and science. This was about having to face the boy who made me want to take my life, and all of his friends.

I had never told my mom the real reason why

all this happened. I thought that maybe it would sway her to my side and help her understand why I wanted this so bad, but I was wrong. "How could you just let someone hurt you like that?" I was met with anger and screams, not the compassion I was looking for, and that resulted in four days of constant arguing in my house. I had worked too hard to better myself for it to get thrown away. I wasn't going back to that school. I didn't care what my mother or father said.

After four days of back and forth arguing, my mom finally gave in to letting me drop out. Under the condition that I would get my GED and continue my education at my local community college. That very same night she had the audacity to call my aunt and tell her that she never doubted me for a second, and she was so proud and happy for me. What a liar! She sat there for a week ridiculing me, telling me how, no child of her's would be a drop out. Now she wanted to act all proud and supportive? I was enraged! I couldn't just sit there and hold back my anger, I had to say something. And of course when I did she denied it all, she turned it into this gigantic argument, and I was fed up. I went off on her, and I wasn't even realizing what I was actually saying. I just let everything out, she did nothing to make any of this easier on me. She swore up and down that she loved me an accepted me, but never once did a single thing to prove it. she was total hypocrite.

Their disapproval and negativity continued on up until the night I turned eighteen. We had a small little party for me, and that night, when everyone was sleeping, I snuck downstairs, took the last piece of birthday cake left on the counter, and left. I wrote a note telling them that I was gone and there would be no use in trying to find me. I knew they wouldn't anyways, because in those prior weeks before, they'd made it very obvious I was a burden. I just left, like a gust of wind, I was gone.

If there is one thing I regret in life, it's that I never told them off. That's why I thought Connor was so brave, because he had done something I could not. Now, I know telling off a random waitress and your parents are two different things, but I was ready to pay the bill and walk out without saying anything about it. For the rest of that day, I would have thought about that woman and what she said, but Connor, he spoke his truth. Speaking my truth was what I wanted to do, but found so hard to accomplish. All that day did was just make Connor more admirable.

Chapter 12
POV Connor

I didn't think I'd see Alex again, and I wouldn't have blamed him. What I did was wrong, and could have ended very badly. I mean, I was only doing it out of love, but sometimes, we get so blinded by love we don't see what we're actually doing. All I saw was some lady attacking Alex and I, the boy I loved. I didn't see all the other people there who could have said or done something. I didn't think about what I'd do if someone decided to defend her, and it got violent. I had no intentions of that, but some people are just looking for an excuse to start trouble like that.

All it takes is just one hateful, irritable, short-tempered person and for me to be at the wrong place at the wrong time and I could be in a heap of trouble. I guess it's just a reality I need to face, and I wasn't used to that. For the most part, I've always hidden my sexuality in public. I put on my 'straight mask' when I go out. I dress in regular jeans and plain t-shirts. I avoid saying certain words and doing certain things so that I can come off as a straight guy. With Alex, I couldn't do that. It's impossible to hide being gay when you're out on a date with your boyfriend. I mean there are ways, but I think it would be unfair to ask that of Alex.

My point is that I'm impulsive and protective, and that causes me to jump up and say things without really thinking about what I'm actually saying. I guess that's why I made such a big scene out of it. I was just upset because I didn't get a chance to explain to Alex what happened. He probably was thinking I was some hot head who had anger issues and a short temper. I just wished I could see him and explain to him what really happened. That I didn't do it out of anger, but for love, but it was too late.

It had been a couple of weeks since the event, and Alex hadn't texted me or called me at all. At this point, I had gone into a total depression. My place was a mess, trash on the floor, take-out containers everywhere, the bed unmade, and I myself looked like a train wreck. I had the same t-shirt on for three days, and I just had no energy to do anything. I just laid in bed watching TV, except I couldn't actually focus on what was going on because all I could think about was Alex and how I messed it up.

I heard a knocking on my apartment door, and I thought it was the UPS guy dropping off another package so I just let it go. After a couple minutes, they knocked again. I groaned as I threw on an old bathrobe and went to the door, with one sock on and the other god knows where. I looked through the peephole of my apartment door and it was Alex. IT WAS ALEX?

This was either good or bad. I'd either officially get my heart broken, or he'd explain what was going on. The first one seemed the most possible, considering there wasn't an excuse in the world as to why he didn't reach out to me, even if he did lose my number, I left him enough voice messages and texts that he'd know where to call me at.

Nonetheless, I ran all across the apartment picking up all the trash and throwing it in the back of the coat closet. Then to my room I ran.

"One minute!" I yelled as I tried to throw on a pair of sweatpants.

Off came the one sock, and on came a hoodie. On the way, I threw a piece of gum into my mouth, ran my hands through my hair, and paused taking a deep breath before opening the door.

"Hey," Alex said.

"Hi," I replied.

"Can I come in?" he asked.

"Sure," I answered.

I opened the door all the way so he could walk in, and I scanned around to make sure there was nothing odd or out of the ordinary he'd notice. Thank god I'd gotten rid of most of the mess, besides an empty soda bottle I was able to kick under the couch before he could notice.

"We need to talk," he said.

I didn't like that, and the look on his face wasn't a good one either. So, I sat down on the couch across from him and prepared myself for my heart to be ripped out of my chest.

"I'm sorry for going all ghost on you, but I needed to figure some stuff out," Alex started.

"No worries. I mean I'm not gonna lie, I was a little concerned, but I get it," I said.

"I should have talked to you. If this is going

to work we have to be open with each other," he continued.

"'This' as in us?" I questioned.

"I mean, if I didn't screw it up already, I'd love nothing more than to be your boyfriend," he answered.

"No, not at all. If anything, I screwed it up with that whole cafe thing," I shyly said.

"Are you kidding, that was the bravest thing I'd ever seen!" Alex reassured me.

"You're serious? Cause I thought you hated me," I said.

"No! I, um, had some stuff to work out at home," he said.

"Well, if you need to talk, I'm here," I reassured him.

"Thanks, but I'd rather just forget all about it if that's okay." he said back.

"Yeah of course, I don't want to pry" What could he have meant by that? I really wanted to ask more questions, but I knew that it wasn't any of my business. When the time was right he would tell me if he wanted me to know.

"Do you want anything to eat? I was getting ready to order Thai?"

"No thanks, I'm good," Alex said.

"You sure? I'd enjoy the company," I insisted.

"I guess I can stay for a little," he replied.

We ordered the food. I got Coconut Curry Noodle soup, which tasted as good as it sounds, and he got Thai Red Curry Chicken. We ate dinner and watched the movies, which was kind of a personal joke I had with myself. You see, when I first moved in, the previous owners had accidentally left a box of their stuff in the closet in the laundry room, and in there was this whole collection of the movies. That night, I stayed up until three in the morning all by myself eating ice cream out of one of those big gallons. I told myself that when I had a boyfriend, I'd make him watch them all with me. Crazy to think that here I was finally doing that. I honestly was beginning to give up on the idea that I'd have any of those special moments, I guess sometimes you just have to be a little patient.

I had this whole list of things I'd written down when I was single that I thought I'd never get to do. Like make a pillow fort out of the couch cushions, bake cookies, but not like those stupid ones that come in a tube that you pop in the oven. I mean like from scratch cookies, where you had to wear an apron and use a rolling pin. I even bought matching aprons for the occasion. I wanted to laugh until I cried, and just have an unforgettable night. That night was my unforgettable night. The night I'd look back on and think, 'wow what a night!' for the rest of my life.

Alex and I wound up crashing on the floor at about five, and woke up the following afternoon with my leg wrapped around his. His elbow was jabbing my ribs, and my head was buried in his side. We both had cookie crumbs all in our hair from rolling over in the night onto the dish which we'd accidentally left on the floor. It was nothing like in the movies where the actors wake up from sleeping, looking all perfect, and their hair combed real neat. We were a total mess, our hair all messy and standing up. Alex had his shirt completely rolled up so that you could see half his stomach, and one pant leg was rolled up all the way above his knee, while the other was down by his ankle. I was first to wake up, but I guess he's a light sleeper because the second I made the slightest noise, he jumped up.

I offered him breakfast, but he said he was good, and that he'd take coffee. I didn't have any though because I hate it and I don't get many guests, so he had to settle for orange juice. I had a bowl of cereal, and I went to the bathroom to brush my teeth and try and make myself look halfway decent. When I came back out, I saw Alex halfway out the door with all his things. I grabbed the door and shut it before he could actually get out.

"Where are you going?" I questioned him.

"I'm sorry but I just can't do this, you're too good for me," he said, holding back tears.

"What are you talking about?" I asked.

"You don't deserve to be with someone like me," he said again.

"What's that mean?" I asked again.

"I lost my apartment, and my job. I have nothing," he replied.

Chapter 13
POV Alex

When I left my parents house, I had nothing. I made minimum wage, which was $15.00 an hour. Working a thirty-two hour work week, bringing home $480.00 a week, without tax being taken out. Adding all that up, my monthly income before tax was $1,920.00. I moved in with some stoner kid who I found online. My rent was $500, and another $100 for utilities. I had a phone bill of $85. That left me with next to nothing to pay for my car and insurance, health insurance, gas money to get to and from work, groceries, and all the other stuff that comes up in between. I was barely skating by, and it had been like that for the past couple years.

Well, that day with Connor in the cafe would sure turn out to change all that. After he told the waitress off in the restaurant, apparently some of the other bystanders recorded the whole thing. They captioned it, "Gays Gone Wild" The thing with social media is that it's so easy to manipulate people's words. Even though Connor was right to do what he did, all these people were being tricked into thinking he was wrong to say what he said. I can't say that any of this didn't bother me because it did, but I wasn't the one being attacked, and as far as I knew Connor didn't even know the video existed. I decided not to show him because what he didn't know couldn't hurt him. I figured the less he knew the quicker we could both just put that behind us. That was until someone by the name 'Username54546' commented, "hey, that kid on the left works at Jenny's. That small boutique shop on fifth street." I was wearing my uniform, so it was obvious he was telling the truth. The video then got sent to the HR team, and I lost my job for 'violating the company's values and ideas.'

When I couldn't pay the rent that next week, my roommate kicked me out. My phone got shut off because I hadn't paid the bill the month before. Then this all happened in the beginning of the month, so I only had like ten hours put in; meaning my final check was next to nothing. I was forced to sleep in my car, but even that became a problem when I couldn't pay the payments and it got repossessed. I was on the streets for two weeks before I decided I'd go to Connor. I had no pride in doing so, and I was really ashamed, but maybe he'd let me stay with him until I got on my feet.

I knocked on his door and I rehearsed what I was going to say. After my first knock, I figured he knew it was me, and was just blowing me off, but something told me to knock again, so I did. Still no answer. Just as I was about to turn around and walk away, I heard footsteps walking towards the door. I wanted to turn and dart away but I had to at least explain myself. When he opened it, I expected him to slam it in my face. After all, I did just ghost him for like three weeks, but instead, he welcomed me in. I could tell he hadn't taken it well because he had chocolate all over his lips and nose. I felt bad asking him, but I had no choice, it was that or living on the street.

I started to talk, but before I could even get it out, he was apologizing for standing up for me, and I couldn't tell him. I mean, he was already blaming himself. What would he do if I told him I was homeless because of it. No, I couldn't. I know I said I wouldn't lie, but I had to this one time. I'd get through this without his help. I'd gone through a lot worse before, this was nothing.

As the night went on, I only felt worse. He insisted I stay for dinner, and from there, we lost track of time having fun together. I seemed to forget about all of my problems and worries. We laughed hysterically as we both goofed around with some funny glasses he'd found in a box. We had such an amazing night, it was like if a romance novel came to life. You could just feel the love we had for each other. As stupid as this sounds, I had butterflies in my stomach the whole night. When I was younger and lived at home, I would lay awake at night thinking about what life would be like when I finally had a boyfriend, and this was it. My dreams did come true. This was the feeling I dreamt of feeling for so long, and it felt great.

At around three or four we both crashed, and I slept really well, the best I'd slept in a long time. Even when I was home, my roommate was blasting his music at all hours, or talking to himself while he was intoxicated. It felt good to feel safe and just let go for once. However, like most mornings, I jumped up out of bed from a dead sleep after having a bad dream. Most of the time I dream about my parents or school, but this time it was this horrible dream where I was in a strange apartment. I didn't know where I was, but it was dark, and I was alone. I heard a rustling in the corner and I froze as I got goosebumps. I wanted to run away, but I was physically stuck. My legs and arms locked in fear of what unknown villain lurked in the shadows. Out of the corner of my eye, I could see a steak knife sitting on the counter. I quickly grabbed it and started walking backwards towards the door, so I could face the intruder. I hadn't seen whatever it was, but I got that feeling that I was being watched. I walked all the way until my back hit the door, and when I turned to open it, I heard footsteps rapidly approaching. I turned to see a person running full speed at me. I stuck out the knife and they fell to the ground instantly. There was blood everywhere, and I knew and I felt like I wanted to vomit. The person on the ground had a mask on so I couldn't tell what they looked like. When I lifted it up, it was Connor.

When I woke up, I was so happy that he was still alive and it was nothing more than a dream, but I also knew that dream was a sign. A sign that I'd ruin his life if I stood around, so while he was in the other room I tried to sneak away, but he caught me. I knew what I was doing, and that I should have just been honest with him, but what else was I to do? Was I to tell the truth even if it means hurting someone I loved, or lie to spare them the pain? Or what if lying would have hurt them even more than the truth? What options did I have that would not end up with Connor getting hurt?

If I told him, he'd beat himself up over it. However, if I just walked away, he'd be stuck with that never ending question of 'why,' and that was the last thing I wanted. I'd been through that with Zach. Thinking I wasn't good enough because there wasn't any other logical reason in my mind as to why we didn't work out, and I didn't want Connor to go through that.

When you make a decision, it's typically a good and a bad choice. Like when you're on a diet and you want ice cream. It's simple, your options are to give up the diet and gain weight, or stick to it and lose weight. However, what if you have two really bad options? What if both options are equally as bad, and you can't pick the 'better' option because there isn't one. What do you do then?

"Where are you going?" Connor asked.

"I'm sorry, but I just can't do this. You're too good for me," I said, holding back tears.

"What are you talking about?" he questioned.

"You don't deserve to be with someone like me," I answered.

"What's that mean?" he asked.

"I lost my apartment, and my job. I have nothing," I said shamefully.

"What? Are you okay?" Connor asked concerned.

"I will be," I replied.

"You can stay here as long as you need," he said without hesitation.

Why was he being nice to me? I wanted him to chase me away, or get mad. Something. I ghosted him for three weeks, was about to leave for good, and he offered me a place to stay?

"No I can't do that," I demanded.

"Of course you can! I'd enjoy the company," he responded.

"I don't even have enough money to pay you rent, I have nothing," I said shyly.

"Don't worry about that. All I ask is that for Valentine's Day, you buy me one of those giant teddy bears. I've wanted one since like the eighth grade. Buy me one of those and we'll be even," Connor smiled.

How could I even think about walking away from someone so amazing? He was the first person ever to actually really care about me, and not because he had to or felt inclined to, but because he wanted to.

"You know what I said about being honest earlier?" I said.

"Yeah?" he questioned.

Me: "I haven't told you why I lost my job," I said.

"What happened?" Connor asked.

"Someone recorded the day at the cafe and they twisted the whole story around to make us look like bad guys. Somehow the video got to HR, and because I was in my uniform, they let me go to avoid a lawsuit or some stupid stuff," I came clean.

Chapter 14
POV Connor

My entire life I've been oppressed. My father has called me a disappointment more times than I can count on five hands. I've been judged by just about everyone I've ever met: teachers, counselors, friends, strangers, and even family. I was bullied for my weight, my acne, my looks, my awkwardness, my lack of friends. In seventh grade some girl threw out her pencil case because I touched it. Freshman year of high school, I sat the whole year alone at a table all to myself. The other kids would all sit crowded together at one small table, simply to avoid having to sit next to me.

I've had things stolen from me, and ripped right out of my hands as I walked down the halls. My phone was once smacked out of my hand, and the whole back was shattered. I had to walk around with long sleeve shirts on for most of the summer because I had gotten jumped in the hallway on the last day of school and I didn't want my parents to see the bruises up and down my arms. I was messaged every day by people telling me how worthless I was and how I'd be better off dead.

I couldn't talk to anybody about it. My parents wouldn't have understood. My counselor at school was of no use to me, I barely even knew her name. I met her once in the beginning of the year, and then again at the end to pick my new schedule.When I did try to make a teacher see what was going on, they'd defuse the situation, but by the next day, things were back to normal. Nothing more than a slap on the wrist, and at home, things were worse.

My father would openly talk about how he feels bad for gay guys because they live a 'lonely life.' He talked about how it's a disgrace to have a gay child, and how if they are going to be gay, they shouldn't talk or post about it, but instead, keep it a secret. Feminine gays, or as he called them 'flamers,' were 'jokes" to him. Every time we'd get into an argument, he'd call me a faggot simply to get under my skin.

My mother was no better. She may not have outright said things like that, but she wasn't good at hiding her facial expressions and her judgement. When I wanted to buy clothes, she'd say things like, "you're going to wear that out?" with a look of disgust on her face. She'd get real quiet and that intense look of sadness on her face if I ever talked about being feminine. I got questioned as to why I didn't have any guy friends, and she'd always ask if I had a girlfriend, even though she knew I was gay. She'd refer to my future partner as my wife, or girlfriend. She'd make it super awkward by asking if I was having sex with any of my friends, even though it was very obvious I wasn't, because they were all girls.

I did not have a supportive life growing up at all. My sexuality was not encouraged, and I was not allowed to be me. I'd cry because I wanted to wear crop tops and put on makeup so badly. I felt so depressed to know my parents would never approve of my future boyfriend like they would a girl. To think of all the people who now suddenly hated me because I wasn't their definition of 'normal' just made me angry.

I was just defending myself. My whole life I have been told I'd never be enough, by friends and family. By the kids in school, strangers online, teachers and professors all alike. Every time I talked about wanting to be a writer and not go to college to become some fancy doctor or lawyer, I'd get this crazy look as if to say, 'are you insane!' I spent too long questioning if I was really good enough, and self doubting. I had this gut feeling that I'd change the world because I was fed up with the hate of this world. It has to change. Yemen, Iran, Brunei, Nigeria, Qatar, Saudi Arabia, Afghanistan, Somalia, Sudan, United Arab Emirates, and Pakistan. All countries where being a member of the LGBTQ+ Community is a crime. Even in many circumstances, it is punishable by death, more specifically, stoning.

I know I was put on this Earth to change this, to speak up and make a difference. The racism, the sexism, transphobia, homophobia, it's all got to end. I will not stop until every person on this planet has an equal opportunity to be themselves and be happy. I'll rest when these ignorant people stop protesting with signs, 'Jesus is anti-gay,' or 'Gay is a sin.' I'll stop when children are loved and accepted by their parents, rather than met with a fist to the face and a lifetime of judgment. I'll be satisfied once Conversion Camps are banned, not just nationally, but globally. I'll be happy when there is not one single person who lays in their bed at night thinking, 'what did I do to be punished like this?'

People can take everything away from you if you let them. From your house and your money, to your hope and your strength, but the one thing they cannot take is your voice. They cannot silence you from speaking your truth and saying what you feel needs to be heard. That right there is more powerful than any bomb or assault rifle. It is more powerful than the world's biggest army, or the toughest fighter. The only way to rise above the hate is to use your voice, because whether you believe it or not, it does have an impact.

No peace treaty or reckoning ever ended by a

result of violence. **All violence does is create more violence.** Violence creates hate and resentment for one another. It creates an endless battle between two parties, both seeking revenge, and with each act, adding more fuel to the fire, eventually leading to the downfall of everyone. I won't stand on a stage and say I hate homophobes and other people like them. I just want to enlighten them because, all it is, is a lack of education.

People don't know what really goes on because we're too scared to share our stories, and I get that. It takes a lot of courage to stand up to the whole world and say, "hey, we need to change!" Now I've never been a courageous person, but I'm going to say it, we need to change! If people really shared their stories, and told their truth, we'd all be disgusted with ourselves. We'd almost certainly be ashamed to call ourselves human beings, and I think that's what we need. The only way to spark change is to speak up and share your truth.

I spoke up that day because I needed to share my story. I truly thought it would do something, but instead, all it got was hate. Here are some of the comments I received:

- "Such a hateful person. These people truly do have some sort of evil in them."
- "If you choose to be gay, you shouldn't get mad when people judge you."
- "What a disgusting world we live in, where two men can openly be in a relationship."
- "People like you should be hung."
- "Disgusting."
- "Disgrace."
- "You give humanity a bad name."
- "My heart goes out to the parents."
- "If you were my son, I'd have disowned you."

Watching that video, and seeing all the hate, I didn't know what to think. It felt like waking up from a really bad dream. I'd spent my whole life convincing myself that I'd speak to crowds of hundreds of people, talking all about equality and injustice, and I had this whole dream, but I guess the world didn't care. My dream was to be an inspiration and to spark change, but in those moments, I felt like change wasn't possible, so I gave up on that. I'd accepted defeat, and just gave into the life that I was born into. I wasn't going to let this break me, but the world wasn't ready to open their eyes, so I wasn't going to waste my breath. I'd focus on what really matters, and that's Alex and I's life together.

Chapter 15
POV Alex

Connor's face went viral real quick. People made memes about him, and the hate comments were unbearable. I mean, he had a lot of people defending him, but it didn't matter. For every one person thanking him for his bravery, there were eight more dragging him through the mud. He changed after that video. I don't know how, but he wasn't the same fiery feisty guy I'd fallen in love with. I mean, don't get me wrong, those following three months were the best three months of my life. I got another job at some burrito place, and we saved up to go on that vacation to Florida like we had planned. We took the typical quirky cute couple pics. We got overpriced bottles of water from the amusement park, and we even got a portrait made of us from some vendor at the beach.

On the drive back, we stopped at the Keys like Connor had planned, and it was incredible. Both of us grew up on the East Coast, so we were used to rough dark water, light brown sand and foamy waves as they crashed on the shore, but not there. The water was crystal clear with barely any waves, and the sand was pure white. They had palm trees on the beach, and it was so well kept with little to no trash anywhere. Back home, there were empty cans and bottles buried in the sand, and paper wristbands littered everywhere. It was a very different experience.

My favorite part was the fish, which neither of us were prepared for. We were out to about our waists when Connor jumped up screaming that something touched his leg. I thought he was over-reacting, until we both looked around and realized we were in the middle of a school of fish. Connor was nearly crying; he was so scared. To this day, we still make jokes and laugh about how Connor nearly peed himself because of some fish.

When we got home, we went furniture shopping, which was quite hilarious given the two of us have totally different styles. Connor is rustic, but I'm modern. I love black, whites, and grays, but Connor would have the whole house brown and beige if you let him. You should have seen the place before I moved in, dark red hand towels in the bathroom, and a beige throw rug in the living room. The whole place was so dull in my opinion, it made me depressed. However, once we got into the store and he saw how pretty a modern apartment could be set up, he changed his mind real quick. We walked in and he gasped; it was his first time in a furniture store. All of his furniture came from the curb, or the goodwill. He was so mind blown by the whole concept of getting to lay on the display beds and try out the couches. He ran over to this one big California King sized bed, and laid down. It was one of those fancy beds that leaned up and down. He was like a little kid trying out all the fancy options on the remote.

Decorating an apartment and going on vacations felt like we were finally starting to have a normal life. We even started using coupons and grocery shopping together. It felt like we had been together for years, when in reality, it was not even a year, but a lot did change in that time. Since the video, I shaved my head and started working out. Connor went back to college to get a liberal arts degree, and also learned to play the saxophone. He wasn't no Kenny G, but he could rock the hell out of those scales. However, he lost his spark, his wittiness, and how he'd always have something to say about something. I mean, he was still funny and smart, and all those things, but something was off. Something about his vibe, like an invisible energy I could sense when I was around him, but I guess we all have our own coping ways. I don't know how I'd react if thousands of people plastered my name across the internet making fun of me. In all honesty, I probably would have been worse than he was.

I couldn't just give up on him like that though. When you love somebody, you can't just walk away. If you can, then you don't love them. I guess that's how you really know if you love someone or not. You can love them when they buy you flowers and bring you on dates, but what happens when they get sick and need someone to rub vapor rub on their chest, or someone to help them when they are feeling down? That's the ultimate test of true love. Relationships are not all pretty, like in romance novels. You've got to get comfortable with sharing a shower and seeing their hair in the drain, and sleeping next to them while they breathe on your neck. You aren't always all dressed up and everything like on dates either. I'll never forget the first time I saw Connor in his cartoon boxers. He has this habit of late night snacking and I happened to walk in on him one night. His hair was all messed up and he was sitting there practically naked eating cereal. It was funny, but it sure wasn't the Connor I was used to. The Connor who had four drawers in his dresser just for shirts.

Don't even get me started on all of his annoying habits. Connor loved a hot place, he hated being cold. He'd rather walk around shirtless with shorts and have all the fans blowing on him than put the air conditioning below 75°F. On the other hand, I loved the cold. I love the feeling of laying on the couch snuggled with a blanket, the electric fireplace going, drinking hot chocolate with a good movie and fuzzy pajamas. It's those little differences where you both have to learn to make sacrifices, and learn to be compatible with each other, because let me tell you, living with another person is not easy.

You better get used to all sorts of annoying stuff, like arguing over who didn't replace the toilet paper when they were finished with the roll, and who lost the house keys. My personal favorite was figuring out what we were gonna cook for dinner. Every night it was a twenty minute debate on whether we wanted Italian, or seafood, or Mexican, or Chinese, and then arguing on who gets to clean the mess up. There are so many nights where I just wanted to bang his head against the counter top out of frustration, but that's what love is. You get mad at each other, but you always make it work out. It might not be right away, it might take two weeks, but eventually, it all works out.

Connor and I were lucky because we didn't really have that many fights. I think the biggest fight we had was when Connor had gone full blown self pity mode on me. We were eight months into the relationship and Connor was still sulking about the whole incident with the video. He had no long term goals, he became content with his little life. He had just given up, and I knew he had so much more potential. He was wasting his talent, he was meant to be his own boss, to rise above his small one bedroom apartment and make something of himself. Now, I get it that it was kind of a big deal and that he needed time to sort out his feelings, but there comes a time when sadness turns into self pity, and that's where Connor was at. He became so nasty and bitter, constantly mumbling and complaining about how nothing mattered. Anytime I would bring something up, he'd brush it off as if nothing felt important to him anymore, and that's when I snapped.

"I don't know what's gotten into you, but you need to stop this pity party! You need to get up, take a shower, get dressed, and go do something with yourself! You need to get over it! It's done, it's over with, you've had more than enough time to deal with it!" I yelled.

He just gave me this look. A look of surprise, followed by a dirty look. His eyes got really narrow and he just rolled over trying to ignore me. I was the wrong person to do that too.

"Just go away," he mumbled.

I should have laughed, because if anyone knows me, they know that I just don't walk away when I see someone needs my help. However, at the time, I was enraged. I was pissed because when I first met Connor, all he talked about was how his dream was to change the world, and now he just gave up because he got a couple of hate comments. I was mad that he could have just given up on himself like that, because I knew he had the capability to do more; he was a born leader. I knew he could help so many people, and to see him lying in bed, half given up, annoyed me because it was selfish. He was giving up because he got called a couple names. What about the kids out there who are abused? The kids who are put into therapy to 'fix' them? The kids who are beaten and attacked every day for just wanting a normal life? He'd forgotten about them.

I got so mad that, without even thinking, I went into the kitchen, filled a big pot with ice cold tap water, and ran into the room. Without even thinking about it, I dumped it on his head.

"What the hell!" Connor yelled.

"Get up! I told you I'm not just gonna give up on you!" I yelled back.

He just sat there soaking wet, water droplets dripping from his hair down to his forehead and running down his cheeks. Without saying any-thing, he got up and walked out of the room. I heard the shower faucet turn on and the water start running. I knew I pissed him off, so to make him feel better, I made his favorite food: crab dip.

It was my aunt's recipe and I'm not sure where she got it from, but it was amazing. I swear she could have sold that stuff in a store, it was so good.

When he finished the shower, he was so mad, he walked right past the food and just plopped on the couch.

"You gonna eat?" I asked.

He didn't respond.

I knew he'd come along, and eventually he did. He just needed time to figure out his own feelings, and work through it himself. When he was ready, the two of us sat down and talked about it. We talked it out, and things slowly became stable again. I would say normal, but it was never normal to begin with. There was always a certain level of chaos in our lives. I was just happy to have my Connor back.

Chapter 16
POV Connor

I felt shattered when that video went viral. I really thought that people would care. Whenever I thought about making a change, I never put any thought into it. I just assumed that, one day, I'd start talking and everyone would listen. I thought that people felt the same way about that kind of stuff. I would never have thought that, maybe if they cared, they wouldn't be blatantly overlooking all of our cries for help, and that broke me. It broke me to think that change may never actually come. All the hope I had, and all the dreams I dreamt were nothing but that; dreams. Dreams that would never come true, and hope for something that would never actually happen.

It was that hope that drove me to do what I did. It was the reason I got out of bed everyday. The only reason I kept fighting was because I believed in a better world, and I just had that whole idea shattered in front of me.

What I didn't realize was, just because some people don't care, doesn't mean the rest of the world was thinking the same way. There were still people out there who thought like me, it's just our voices weren't being heard. I realized I couldn't let the hate crush me. I couldn't drown in all the violence. I had to keep fighting to stay afloat. It was a struggle, but I had to.

As mad as I was at Alex, I needed to hear all that.

I needed a slap in the face to call me back to reality. While I was in the shower, I thought long and hard about all the famous people in our world. I mean, what if they gave up? What if they gave up the first time they got rejected? What if, on their first failed attempt, they just gave up on their dreams? I wouldn't know, because they didn't. They fell and they stumbled, but they always kept getting up.

I'm not going to lie, it took me a couple of days before I talked to Alex, but I was ready to get back to who I was. I had a couple ideas in mind that I had been wanting to do but pushed aside, so I figured, why not start there? I told Alex I wanted to throw an LGBTQ+ Prom. I didn't go to prom when I was in high school. What was the point? I wouldn't have been able to take a guy like I wanted to, so I just didn't go.

I wanted to plan this big extravagant prom for all the LGBTQ+ kids who didn't go to prom, or didn't have the experience they would have preferred. For whatever reason, it didn't matter, I just wanted to give them what every straight kid got naturally. There'd be no judgment whatsoever. You could bring whoever you want, wear whatever you want, and just be happy.

When I told Alex, I was sure he'd just dismiss the idea or call it impossible, but he actually took an interest in it. Before I knew it, we were setting up a website for people to send in donations, calling for decorations, and even putting down a deposit for the hall. It was so surreal that something in my head that I'd pictured so vividly was actually coming to life. Everything was coming along exactly like I planned it.

We had a DJ come in and made sure that he had all the right playlists. We had a giant sheet cake that was layered with the colors of the rainbow on the inside, and the top said "be proud." Alex and I made cupcakes, and the icing was in swirls for the trans and bi flag. We had made up gift bags for people to take home with pins and stickers in them. Each centerpiece on the table was a bouquet of rainbow roses, which I didn't think they could do, but they were able to dye the white ones into the colors that didn't come naturally. The table cloths were just pride flags, and we had bought the multi color confetti guns and shot them everywhere so that the entire place was covered in rainbow confetti.

We wanted everyone to know that that night

was supposed to be all about them and their happiness. We wanted people to walk in and say "wow!" I think we did a pretty good job, if I say so myself. I mean, it wasn't exactly perfect, and if money wasn't an issue, we'd have done a lot more, but it didn't matter what it looked like. The message we were sending was what was important, and that message was that gay kids deserve just as much happiness as the straight ones.

We put so much time and effort into that prom, that even if it failed and nobody showed up, it was still all worth it. Alex and I bonded so much in those weeks of planning. I really knew that he was the one. He knew just how to handle me, and what to say. He knew how to distract me when I was overthinking something stupid.

He would always do small things for me, like picking a cute flower off the ground and bringing it home. Or, surprising me with milkshakes if I felt overwhelmed. He'd come home with a card and a box of candy just because he wanted me to know how much he loved me. He made me feel special and important.

I'd never been important to someone before. For the most part, I was always just there. I was never the first, or even the second option. Alex made me realize that I mattered. I had spent so much time telling people that they were important, but I was ignoring my own advice. I wouldn't have taken any of that time back.

No matter what happened, I knew Alex would never leave my side. That gave me a sense of security that no lock and key could ever give me. I still had my doubts though, and the days leading up to it were super stressful. However, I was fortunate enough to have the man of my dreams at my side. To wake up every morning to his sleepy face would have me sitting there smiling, thinking how lucky I was to have him in my life. To wake up and be able to do what I love, with the love of my life, was a rare thing not many people have the privilege to get to do. Yet, there I was, living my dreams. Except, this time, they were real. I could feel them with such a burning intensity.

I had it all under control until the night of the event. That's when it really hit me hard. Everything was scheduled to start at seven, and there I was at ten to seven all dressed up, waiting for Alex to come out so we could both open the doors together. I was nervous, scared, and happy, all at the same time. I thought about my past, and how two years ago, I didn't know if I'd ever be happy. I remembered back to when I would sit there for hours crying, just wishing things would change, and not knowing how I would ever get out of the pain. The pain of uncertainty, and not knowing if things would ever get better. That's when I was reminded of why I was doing what I was doing, because so many people don't have hope, and the not knowing can eat you alive. That night, I was showing all those people that it does get better, that it does change. It can't, and it won't always be bad. It has to get better.

I was on the verge of tears when I was completely taken back when I saw Alex. My back was turned to the door as I fixed myself in the mirror. When I heard the tapping of his shoes as he came into the room. I looked up, and there he was, all dressed up with his rainbow suspenders. He had his hair all combed back, and he just slowly walked over to me smiling. He then looked at me and started laughing. I didn't even have to look, I knew it was the crooked bow-tie. He just continued to laugh as he turned me around and unclipped it, straightening it the right way and placing it back on. When he turned me around, we made eye contact for a split second and I felt my heart melt. He fiddled with it for a couple seconds, and finally, he got it.

"You ready?" I asked him.

"Uh, yeah. One second. I forgot something," he answered.

He walked out of the room and came back a couple seconds later with a big sign in his hands. It was white with all different colored designs on it. Little dots and spirals to give it that vivid energetic vibe. He drew a mini pride flag with a heart in the middle of it, and in big letters, he had written, 'will you go to prom with me?'

"I never really asked you, but will you be my date to prom?" Alex asked.

I struggled to even say anything. I was so taken back. Then finally, I happily shouted "YES!!"

I hugged him and I didn't want to let go. All of it was because of him. I wouldn't have been there that day if it weren't for him and his support. He was the reason I smiled and laughed. The reason I believed in a better world. He gave me hope.

So, together, the both of us holding hands, walked across the dance floor past all our decorations and hard work to the front doors, and we stopped. We took a deep breath, and together, we said in unison, "I love you." Then, we opened the doors. I don't know what I was expecting, but it wasn't that. A crowd unlike anything I'd ever seen, and not one frowning face.

Everyone was just happy, and not that fake happy. That real genuine happiness. You could tell they all felt safe, and like they belonged. Something most of them probably never felt before. It felt so good to help all of them, especially once I started talking to them and I heard some of their stories. My heart broke to hear some of the things they had to say. Nobody should ever feel invalidated for who they are, and so many people are. The amount of people out there right now, sitting there all alone feeling helpless, how do we make this world a better place for them? The answer was easy: we stand up to the hate, we rise above the petty violence and name calling, and we demand a real change, and that started with me.

Chapter 17
POV Alex

The prom was a success. It was more than a success. It was the beginning of what would turn into something unimaginably extraordinary. That night, seeing all those teens and young adults filled with so much happiness and excitement did something to both Connor and myself. It changed us because we realized that we have the power to literally change peoples lives.

Talking to some of those kids, they told us stories of things they had to endure, and told us all about how that night would be something that they'd never forget. You could see the happiness in their eyes. How, if they could've just froze time and stood there forever, they'd have done it, and it was all because of us. I wondered how many more lives we could impact and change, so I got to talking with Connor, and we decided to step up our role in changing things.

We started planning protests. It wasn't supposed to be much, but we just wanted people to be comfortable with sharing their stories, and we wanted them to know that they are never alone, because both of us had known that feeling all too well. When you feel like that, you do stupid thing, things you don't want to do, but you do them anyways because you're desperate for a solution to end the pain: drugs, alcohol, sex, lying. Eventually when none of that works, because I'd know, I tried it all, that's when you get really desperate and you decide one day that you're just done.

You plan it all out, how you're gonna end it all. You try to tell people subtly what's happening, but they don't pick up on it, and then you do it. You take your life, and not everyone is as lucky as I am to have been saved and recovered. So this was important to me, because I was proof that things get better.

At first, we had a small following; a couple people, maybe a dozen or so. We'd plan a spot and camp out for a couple hours holding up signs, trying to bring awareness to some of the stuff going on in the world. We weren't pushy or anything, we just wanted people to be a little more aware of some of the issues going on. We wanted people to sign our petitions to add LGBTQ+ History into the school curriculum's. We wanted people to know that, statistically, gay teens are **four** more times likely to take their life than straight teens.

We wanted them to see the alarming statistics of substance abuse amongst gay teens, and we wanted them to know that this was all directly caused by how society treats us as a group, and as individuals.

As we got bigger, so did our goals. We had about fifty people show up to one of our protests outside of the state capital demanding for more LGBTQ+ support groups in our schools and local areas. A safe place for gay teens to go and vent and just feel welcomed. Exactly like the prom we planned; a judgment free zone where everyone is invited to be themselves.

If you're anything like me, school was a nightmare. I got bullied and couldn't do anything about it. I mean, I could have gone to the counselor, but in reality, what could she have done? I mean, she might have reprimanded one of the kids, but how could she reprimand twenty kids, and what would have stopped them all from just coming back and doing worse things? You can't just avoid those issues, because for every one bully, there's ten more of his/her friends waiting to jump you. So, unless they wanted to create some sort of LGBTQ+ only school, we needed some sort of safe place. So many kids go to school, get bullied, go home, get told how to act, and are forced to suppress who they are, and that's just their life.

There isn't an escape from the cruel world we live in. The bullying and the hate is everywhere: online, in school, in our houses, in stores. There is no escape for us, and that's part of what we were trying to fight for. Before we knew it, we had five hundred people supporting us and joining our fight for equality.

Our protests soon became big. Every time we had one, we set new records. We were growing so fast, because so many people believed in what we were saying, it's just they were intimidated to share what they were feeling. They thought they were the only ones who felt like that, or they were the only ones going through it. Once they realized that they weren't alone, we were unstoppable. We weren't playing any more games. We were done dealing with the phony politicians that would walk onto those stages and say all these things about how they support equality for all, but never actually did anything to change things.

When black trans women were hung from trees all across the country, these fake politicians stood up there and said how disgusting and wrong it was, but didn't actually do anything to change it. So, in my eyes, they were a part of the problem, because they had the power to change it all. They could create laws, and actually fix our broken society, but instead, they sat there not doing anything about it. Enough was enough! We were tired. Tired of dying, tired of feeling pain. Fed up with the fact that, just because we weren't straight, our whole life was ten times harder than everyone else's.

Being loved, accepted, confident, happy, all things that most straight people are born with, but us gays have to fight everyday just to feel like we matter. Change should have been made the very first time someone took their life, directly because of their sexuality. Change should have come when we spoke up about the violent acts going on, but instead, we were just basically left to deal with it. We were tired of being let down, neglected, and ignored, so we didn't care if we had to stand there every day in the hot, cold, rain, or wind. We were not going anywhere. You were not silencing us. Not anymore.

We became leaders to something far greater than us. A movement bigger than anything we'd ever imagined. We weren't just fighting for the people there at that moment, but for the thousands of people in the past who were imprisoned, killed, beaten, and abused for their sexuality. We were fighting so that their sacrifices weren't in vain. We were fighting for the gay kids who were unborn, in a hope that one day, they would be seen the same as straight kids. A future where nobody cries themselves to sleep because they aren't straight. A future where everyone is seen as a person, and not by their sexuality, gender, or color of their skin.

Was it uncomfortable and scary at times? Of course it was, but bravery was something we had to adapt to and learn. There were plenty of days where people would curse at us, and throw their garbage towards us. We had people who would stand right across from us with big signs that quoted bible verses in an attempt to make us feel guilty, but you learn to not let that stuff get to you. When you truthfully believe in something, it doesn't matter what anyone else says or does, nothing will stop you. When a group of people have been suppressed for so long and they've finally said enough is enough, nothing is going to get in the way of them achieving their goal. All the fighting and struggling, just to be treated with basic human decency makes you strong. Stronger than any professional fighter or boxing champion. It gives you charisma, and a cause to believe in. If people believe in something enough, they'll give their life to support it. Equality isn't that drastic of an idea that most people wouldn't back us.

Straight, gay, trans, bi, Black, White, Hispanic, or Asian; we're all people, and all we wanted was to be treated and seen like that. Our cause and our beliefs were easy to back, and because of that, within the next month, we became trending everywhere. People looked up to Connor and I. There was one protest in particular that really changed it all for us, and opened my eyes as to what we truly meant to these people.

We were protesting the use of conversion therapy outside, across the street from this one church that was practicing it. We had about three hundred people there with us. Connor and I were upfront. These events got very hectic, so we didn't really get to witness a lot of the stuff that was happening. Everyone is chanting and yelling, and you've got the police there for crowd control making sure the event doesn't turn ugly. The line was so long by this point that we couldn't actually see where it ended, just an endless wave of pride flags and posters. Out of the corner of my eye, I saw this young boy who had to be no older than sixteen. He was walking with his family, and they were covering his eyes to shield him from us. You could tell the mother and father were disgusted by their facial expressions, and you could tell the kid was upset.

He had that look and that walk, that I myself used to have. He just looked tired, walking slouched over with his head tilted towards the ground. Just as they reached the door, this young man broke free from his father's grip and ran towards us. I remember thinking how sad it was that he had to find refuge in a total group of strangers, and that his own parents had let him down. In those moments, that's when I knew that we were fighting for a real and true cause.

It wasn't long before the cops stepped in and took him back to his parents, but for a split second, he felt like he belonged somewhere. I could tell by the way his face lit up, and the passion in his stride as he ran towards us. To think about him, and what he'd have to go through, I couldn't just give up on him. I broke free from the group and ran across the street, jumping over, and dodging between the police and their makeshift barricade. Then out of nowhere, I looked back and several officers were coming right at me, ready to take me down.

I just froze. I knew I couldn't escape it, so I just stood there, waiting for them to come and put me in handcuffs. But, before I knew it, I was surrounded. Not by the police, but by our supporters. They all made a circle around me and the boy, pushing away all the officers with their bare hands. I knew I didn't have much time, so I just hugged him, and he broke down. That's an intense feeling, to have someone else in your arms sobbing on your shoulder and you can't help them. I just did what I could and stood there, holding him for as long as he needed me to. "It'll get better, stay strong," I said, trying not to cry myself.

Chapter 18
POV Connor

Our protests gave hope to a lot of people. Our words, although they were just words, inspired people. Even though we were doing a lot of good, it was also taking over our lives. I was worried about

Alex, he was taking this whole thing too seriously. The hard part about what we were doing was that we couldn't save everyone, and Alex was trying to do exactly that. It almost cost him everything we had been working so hard to build up.

We were out protesting one day when we saw this one kid. I mean, my heart melted for the kid, but there was nothing we could have done, besides what we were already doing. Alex, I guess, couldn't just let that kid walk away. He has a big heart, and it always blocks the logic part of his brain. He makes decisions and does things based on his feelings, which isn't a bad thing, but sometimes it can cause a lot more trouble and problems than what you intended.

We had always made sure that everyone knew our protests were peaceful. I know that everyone was angry, but being calm was the most important part. We needed these people to not only hear us but respect us, and yelling and screaming would only push them further away. We need to have civil discussions, not heated arguments. The more angry we got, the more they'd push back, so staying calm was very important.

Alex didn't know how to stay calm, he only

knew how to stand up for what was right. He impulsively decided that he'd single-handedly save that boy. Without any warning, before I could even stop him, he was gone. He had dropped his stuff and taken off, straight for the line of police that separated us from that church.

The whole thing was a ticking time bomb ready to explode. You had hundreds of angry people on our side who were tired, exhausted, and angry. Along with the fact that most of them had personal connections to the cause, which only intensified their feelings. Then you had hypocritical bullies and antagonizers on the other side. In between both of us were the police. The police were also worn thin because they had to put up with the heckling from both sides. Everyone was waiting for an excuse to explode.

When Alex took off, he was the spark that lit the situation on fire. Either he forgot he was a leader, or lost track of reality, because when he took off, it was pure and total thoughtlessness. The intentions were there, but the process in which he was going about it could have cost us everything. It wasn't only him who broke the rule, but a dozen others did as well. It was a full on brawl, yet at the same time, it was also so beautiful. To see unarmed men and women standing up against police, fist to baton, all because they believed in our cause. That's when I realized what this truly was, and the power that we had.

In those moments, I felt so empowered. I myself forgot about the rules and joined right in with them. We were all in this big circle around Alex holding them off. They tried using their batons and their bodies to get through, but there were just too many of us. It was like our faith in a better world gave us super powers, because I, still to this day, don't know how we did it, but we did. The stand off of a lifetime.

Obviously, they called for back up right away and wanted to defuse the situation as quickly as they could, but we held our ground. Time seemed to slow down for those two minutes. I was holding back with everything I had. I dug my feet into the ground and pushed with all my strength.

When their back up came, we all knew it was over. Between the tear gas and the shields, we didn't stand a chance. We were everyday people who were not trained for that kind of stuff. It was a hopeless fight. Even with that in mind, most of us stood our ground until the end, but once one of us fell, they were able to just swarm right in and make their way over to Alex. I tried to warn him, but it was too late. He'd fallen to the ground, and the kid was lost in the chaos of people running and coughing from the smoke. My eyes were watering, and I could barely breathe, but I managed to crawl over to Alex, who was unconscious. I remember the first thing I thought was 'please don't be dead.'

I didn't actually get a chance to check, because these two gorilla sized arms wrapped around me and dragged me away. I was kicking and screaming, but it was useless. I was carried all the way to the back of a cop car. I mean, it was all sorted out, and nobody was charged or anything, but all I was worried about was Alex. I'd seen him fall, but that was it. For all I knew, he could still be laying there, or worse. So as soon as they said I was good to go, I rushed back to the spot where it happened. There wasn't anyone there, just several ambulances and cop cars. I looked all around and saw no signs of him. I knew he wasn't gone, he couldn't have just disappeared. I was so scared, I went into panic mode and I just couldn't help myself. I was shaking and sweating as I searched every nook and cranny in that whole place. Behind the church, in the bushes, the dumpsters. He was nowhere to be found.

I was at my wits' end searching for him, and I guess this EMT saw how troubled and distraught I was, because she came over to me and asked if everything was okay. I was barely able to speak, my voice was shaking, and the back of my throat felt scratchy and itchy as I tried to explain what happened. I, myself, still couldn't process it. How could he just be gone? After calming me down, she told me she'd do her best to see what happened, but I didn't really feel assured. I just sat there, sipping on the small water bottle she gave me, taking deep breaths while trying to stay calm.

As soon as I saw her come back, I jumped up. Before I could even ask if he was okay, she had answered my question.

"I found your boyfriend. He's safe. We've treated him for some minor complications, but overall he's fine," she told me.

She offered to bring me to him, so I followed. Her name was Kayla. She had this amazing aura where she could just naturally emit soothing energy. I'll never forget her, even to this day, I think about her. I wonder if she ever became a nurse like she had talked about, or maybe she found herself on a new path. It really makes me think, when I look back on all the people I've come across, and wonder where they might be now, all these years later. Believe it or not, those small conversations help. Showing basic human decency, and common courtesy goes a long way in today's world. Especially then, I mean I was losing it searching for him, I wasn't level headed or thinking clearly. It was her kindness that brought me back to reality. If it weren't for her, who knows if I would've freaked out and done something stupid, or had a panic attack and not been able to be there for Alex when he needed me the most. I know those are all 'what if's,' but still, it's crazy to think one person's kindness can extend that much.

When we finally got to Alex, he was slowly waking up from the bash to his head. She warned me of the amnesia, and told me he had a concussion that might take a few days before he was back to normal. I had this big packet filled with symptoms and the do's and don'ts. One of the big issues was headaches, and what would trigger them: loud noises, bright lights, any quick or sudden movements. Stuff I already sort of knew. She gave me pain killers for the pain, which I was skeptical about giving him, but after the first couple of hours, it was almost cruel to let him suffer like that.

I mean, once he was awake he was fine. He didn't remember what had happened, but he was awake and functioning. We went home and were talking on the couch, eating pudding out of those little cups. I could tell he was zoning out, because he seemed distant. He was just looking at the corner, by our ivory plant, not acknowledging me at all, just blatantly staring.

Within seconds, he was completely tuned out from reality. Before I could even try to pull him back, he was on the ground screaming "make it stop!" while holding his ears. I managed to help him to the bedroom, which was a struggle in itself because by that point, he couldn't even stand by himself. I had to lift him up under my arms and allow him to shift all of his weight onto me so he could walk to the room. He started to sweat profusely, and he got pale white. I leaned him up and ran to get a wet rag to cool him off.

I got about an inch away from his forehead and he started to wince in pain. "Ow. Stop, it hurts!" I felt helpless. I didn't know what to do.

I was still skeptical about the pills because, well, they're basically narcotics, so I substituted them for extra strength Tylenol. It had taken fifteen minutes to ease up some of the pain, and only lasted a couple of hours. That's when I realized how senseless it was to not just be giving him the pills that he needed, and that I knew would help him.

After the first dose, he was fine; loopy, but fine. He wasn't screaming, and could actually sit up and eat something. I couldn't turn on the lights yet in the bedroom, just the small lamp on my nightstand, and the TV still bothered him, but I mean he had a concussion. It was all normal, and to be expected.

Gradually, he got better. Within the next three weeks, he was completely back to normal. He was able to use his phone and watch TV. He was up and about doing things like he normally did before, and the whole thing became a distant memory. An experience I'd never forget, but also a thing of the past.

Chapter 19
POV Alex

When I woke up, I didn't remember much. I just felt very weak. It took almost all of my energy just to open my eyes. I was in and out for a little while because, one second I was sitting on the ground, and the next I was in the car, and from there, somehow, I was sitting on the couch. That's when I kind of had that sense of reality come back to me, but I still could just barely make sense of what was going on.

"Are you alright?" Connor asked me.

"Yeah I'm fine," I responded.

"You really scared me there," he said.

"I'm strong and grown. I know how to handle myself," I snapped.

I had a decent idea of what had happened, there were just a few blanks that I couldn't put together. I remembered getting up that day, packing my bag, and bringing all the posters to the car. I remembered getting there, seeing all the people, and thinking how amazing it was that so many people believed in our cause. I don't remember why, but I know something happened because I started to run, and from there, I was woken up by the ambulance.

It was bothering me because I knew something happened and I could feel it right there in the front of my head, but it was all so cloudy I couldn't make sense of it. I kept trying and trying, but it was blocked, and it was annoying. I could remember it, but I couldn't. I remember it happening, but not any of the physical details.

I tried to go back in time and 'relive' the whole event, but it was just all flashing lights and darkness. Like a glitch in my mind, or when the TV goes static, then all of a sudden BAM! I heard sounds. I couldn't see anything. It was super bright, like I was staring at the sun, but I heard noises. Lots of people were screaming. None of it made sense, but I could tell there were a lot of angry people. I felt a sense of danger, like when you're in the dark and you get that eerie feeling that something is watching you. I turned around, but all I saw was blinding light.

I felt a sense of warmth, and I could physically feel as if someone was hugging me, but when I looked, no one was there. Then, all of a sudden, like a ton of bricks, it all hit me. It was like a typhoon. All those blocked memories flooded into my head. I remembered the boy, standing there hugging him, wanting to help him so badly but feeling helpless, and then a sharp pain on the back of my head, and I fell to my knees.

Out of nowhere, this intense pain hit me and I nearly vomited. When I looked around, I was back to the living room, except I was seeing two of everything, and I felt like I was on a roller coaster. Everything was hyper exaggerated, like if someone just pressed fast forward mode on life. I went to get up and the pain got worse, so I just collapsed.

I don't know how I managed to get to the room, but I was in agony. The faster things got, the more my eyes felt like they were gonna pop out of my head. I had this intense pressure that I could feel building up, and my ears started to pop. Everything was spinning. I felt my eyes closing as I got weaker, and weaker, but every time they closed, I felt like I was falling.

It was like that for a couple days, with very few moments in between where my head actually felt normal. Then I took the pain pills, and it all went away, but not just my headaches, all of my problems went away. It was a false reality where I didn't feel insecure or sad. I was just happy and able to let go. For once in my life I was myself. That's when I remembered why I loved getting high all the time when I was younger, and I missed it. I missed the feeling of not caring and just being happy. That was the beginning of my relapse, and I had no idea.

When you start using drugs, you only do it occasionally. Every once in a while you need that little stress reliever to help get you through the day. Then, that every once in a while becomes an everyday thing. I won't lie, being high is the best feeling in the world. It numbs you from everything, it's the crash that makes it hard to deal with. Coming back to the real world where you aren't numb and you actually have feelings that you can't just neglect. That's the hard part. That's the part I always struggled with, because I loved being numb and not feeling anything, especially when my whole life was just one giant train wreck. It always felt good to just sit back and drift away into space.

You also don't realize you have a problem until it's too late and you're already neck deep in what we call addiction. You tell yourself you have it under control, and that you could stop whenever you want, but when you go to stop, you can't. You've become so dependent on it to make you happy, that you literally forget how to function without it. It takes over you, and turns you into a whole new person, and the worst thing is you have no control over it. You're conscious about the things you're doing, and you know that it's all bad: the sneaking, the lying. It's horrible, and not just bad for you, but for the people around you. It eventually gets to a point where drugs are more important than anything else, including the ones you love. Connor would know that better than anyone.

When the thirty day prescription ended, and I was out of 'happiness,' I panicked. I couldn't go back to living my life the way I was. So, I got a second job as a male escort. Now I'm not proud of it, but I needed the money to buy more drugs. I didn't want to steal from Connor. He worked hard, and I was broke, so what was I to do?

I had called this jewelry store, and sold all my watches, and stuff, but that would only get me so far. So I did my research on good paying jobs that paid cash, and this small little bar came up. It was about twenty minutes away from our apartment so I would never run into anyone I knew. My job wasn't easy. I was basically an object. I could be bought for however long they wanted, and I was just theirs. I had devalued myself to nothing more than a sex toy, and all of it was for drugs. Working five hour shifts, laying on a dirty old mattress in the upstairs of a bar, when I could've been at home sleeping next to my favorite person in the world, but the drugs meant more.

I'd get off work, go straight downstairs when my shift ended and order a shot of vodka. Then, walk out back and buy what I needed. For the most part, it was pills and weed. Before I knew it, I was snorting coke in the bathroom where the lights were falling out of the ceiling and the water didn't work from the faucets. I'd go in, lock the door, go over to the sink, make my line, and from there, the rest is self explanatory. I'd pass out, my face laying on the cold, dirty floor that probably hadn't been mopped since the place opened. I'd just lay there, dead. I mean not literally, but mentally I was gone. I'd feel myself drift off, close my eyes, and wake up at five or six and go home. I'd get in bed right before Connor was about to wake up at eight and pretend like I was there all night.

I did that for a long time, and eventually, all the sneaking around and lying became second nature. It wasn't hard to look Connor in the eyes and lie to him, or feel guilty, it was just life. Unfortunately, like all lies, I would eventually get caught. It was our one year anniversary, the one day I could not get high. I had been preparing myself for weeks in advance. I really thought I could do it.

I made reservations for dinner, and I ordered flowers. I wanted to do something cute, but at that time, my mind was so fried I couldn't actually put thought into anything. I knew Connor didn't care about any of that stuff, he wasn't a materialistic person. To him, it was all about the memories and being in the moment. So as long as I showed up sober, and didn't do anything stupid, we'd be all good.

However, I underestimated how hard that was going to be. I had dipped into most of my savings, and sold practically all of my stuff just so I could get high. I had agreed to do a private party to make enough money for dinner, and I planned it all out. Our date was on Saturday, and the party was the Friday before. I showed up to work my regular time and told Connor I'd meet him at the restaurant because I was going to sleep at a friend's house. In reality, I was getting off of work and driving two and half hours to some mansion in this humongous gated community.

Private parties paid a lot because they were mostly all rich people. Important rich people who held powerful positions and couldn't just walk into a strip club or a bar. Lawyers, CEO's, low level politicians, people you'd never expect. They were buying our silence, and the cost of that was $500 an hour, plus tips. They also had to supply the drugs and alcohol.

It was all done anonymously through an app where they'd request who they want and then give you the information on where to go so I had no idea who I was meeting. All I knew was to park my car in the Super Store outside the development and they'd reimburse me for a taxi to get my way in. After that, I was sent GPS coordinates where I was supposed to have the cab driver drop me off. From there, I was explicitly informed to make sure the driver was gone before making my way through a small path in the woods. They said to follow the 'blue ribbons.' I wasn't sure what that meant, but that would bring me to the back gate where they'd be waiting.

The whole thing sounded sketchy, but I was being paid $2,000 so I didn't have the right to complain. I just did what it said, and there I was, at three in the morning, walking through the woods looking for 'blue ribbons.' Nobody was around me, but I still felt creeped out, like I was being watched. I was just about sure I was lost until I saw out of the corner of my eye a glimpse of blue. I turned and ran to a tree. Sure enough, there it was. Just like it had said; a trail of them. I found myself at the edge of the woods and coming up to a huge ten foot wrought-iron fence with lights and security cameras everywhere. I could tell by the size of the house, and the extra security, that this person was very important.

The yard was giant. A three tier pool; the top level being a hot tub, leading off of that, a smaller regular pool, and then from there, the ground level pool being the biggest and the widest. They all had a waterfall connecting them to each other, and the water was crystal blue. On the side was a giant glass storage shed filled with floats, rafts, and other stupid tools. Next to it was a tennis court, and next to that was a sand pit set up for volleyball.

I was admiring how beautiful everything was, when suddenly, all the lights outside cut out and I jumped.

"Hurry up! Hurry! Come on!" a voice yelled from the dark.

I couldn't see who was talking to me, I just heard a kind of general direction, so I just started running towards it. I ran along the fence, following the voice "This way! Almost there!" As I got closer, the outline of a person formed and I saw the gate. I slipped inside just in the knick of time, because as the gate hit, the power turned back on and everything was lit up again. Then I heard a phone ring, and I went to reach into my pocket, but it wasn't mine.

"Yes father, I'm fine. It was just a power outage. Some idiot probably hit a pole or something.....No you don't need to send someone to check up on me....Yes I'm fine....I will....Love you too," he said and hung up the phone. He turned and looked at me smiling. "Jack," he stuck his hand out.

Not gonna lie, he was cute, and he was young;

about my age. He was built, very muscular, and he had curly brown hair that was down to about his ears. He was wearing a muscle shirt and bathing suit bottoms. He must have just gotten out of the pool because he was still dripping wet from his shorts. You could see he hadn't bothered to dry off his top, because it stuck to him like glue, and you could see the whole outline of his figure. His abs, pecs, chest, and shoulders; all of it was visible. He was probably one of the hottest guys I'd ever seen, and I was getting paid to sleep with him.

He took me inside, downstairs into his base-ment/game room. I was browsing his record col-lection on the wall. All these iconic bands. I was looking at thousands of dollars in records all just sitting there collecting dust. There was a bunch of old vintage arcade games, and a big solid oak vintage style bar stocked with top-shelf whiskeys, and other liquors. In the middle of the room was a big pool table, and mounted on the wall was a big flat screen TV. I was standing there taking in how insane this place was when I heard the sound of Jack struggling behind me. Before I could turn around to see what was going on, he flipped. "God dammit. This lighter isn't working!" He slammed it on the table and screamed, not just your typical scream, but a rage filled anger scream. A scream that came from so deep inside of him, you could tell he had a lot bottled up. Without warning, he just started throwing stuff. Papers everywhere, and he flipped the pool table all by himself. He used a stick to bash the whole wall of records. I remember thinking to myself, 'Alex, what did you get yourself into?'

After his little tantrum, he just stood there panting, looking at the mess. He dropped the pool stick and grabbed my hand, pulling me upstairs. I liked how he was controlling of me, how he just told me what to do and took control of everything.

We were now upstairs in his bedroom, which matched the rest of the house. The closet alone was probably bigger than Connor and I's apartment. It looked like the stock room for a store in the mall, because most of the stuff was still sitting there brand new in the plastic with the tags on. He even had his own bathroom, with a giant walk-in shower and a separate Jacuzzi, and the whole thing looked like it was untouched. No dust on any of the windowsill's, not even a wrinkle in the sheets on the bed, it was surreal to me how someone could possibly live like this. "Sit," he said as he pushed me onto the bed. He walked over to his dresser and pulled out a pack of cigarettes. He had an old zippo lighter that he flicked as he lit it. His eyes rolled back into his head a little and he walked over to me.

He pushed himself onto me, and as I fell back onto the bed, he began to take his shirt off. I wrapped my arms around his back while he began to kiss me, slowly but intensely. Then faster, and with each kiss, he got lower and lower from my neck, down my stomach, all the way to my belt. From there it was intense, unlike anything I'd ever felt. Even Connor, as ashamed as I am to admit it, but that was the best sex of my life. It was so good that I'd forgotten about him, forgotten about our one year anniversary, our relationship, everything.

When I woke up the next morning, I must have forgotten where I was, because in a half fogged sleep, I rolled over and cuddled up to who I thought was Connor. Immediately, I knew it wasn't him when I felt his six-pack, and I nearly jumped up. Who was this in my bed? Then I realized, it wasn't my bed, or my house. I laughed it off and tried to leave, but he was already awake.

"Where are you going?" Jack asked me.

"I've got to go home," I said as I was putting on my pants. He got up from under the blankets and walked over to me in his boxers. He hugged me and forced my head back towards his shoulder. He took a deep breath as he rubbed the back of my head. I was so uncomfortable, but I didn't want to move. He had this spell on me.

"At least let me make you breakfast," Jack said.

"No, it's fine. I can get something on the road," I insisted.

"I wasn't asking," he said. "You just wait here. I'll call you when I'm ready."

I couldn't find it in me to speak, so I just nodded my head while trying to process what was going on. He leaned in, putting his thumb on my upper lip and paused. "Good," he said before walking out and shutting the door behind him.

I sat on his bed for a while, bored; just going through his things. He had a lot of trophies on the wall: football, soccer, wrestling, lacrosse, weight lifting. This kid was fit. He had signed letters from congressmen in display frames. I decided I'd get creative in my time. I started trying on all his hats and sunglasses, looking in the mirror, pretending they were mine. I would've killed for his life, he had no problems. He just woke up and did what he wanted. Not a clue what the words 'responsibility,' or 'accountability' meant. He was so nonchalant and unpredictable. I loved it, but it also scared me.

When breakfast came, I was expecting some pop tarts or half raw pancakes. Instead, he called me down to a full table set up: orange juice, waffles, eggs, sausages. He cooked it all. He pulled out my chair, and I sat down where he told me to. Except, there was no knife or fork, and when I went to go grab something, he stopped me.

"I'll get it for you," he insisted.

He was still very mysterious, and I felt something in my gut telling me to leave, but I also knew if I tried, god knows what would happen to me. I just sat there, trying to get an accurate read of the situation, but I couldn't. He was just too closeted, and I liked it. I liked how, when I was with him, I didn't have to think. I was in a bad spot, and to be honest, thinking wasn't my strong suit. I always over-thought everything, spent hours degrading myself, convincing myself I didn't deserve anything good. I liked how he turned me into a zombie.

After we ate, I went to get up. Again, he stopped me.

"Wait," Jack said.

"No, I really have to get going," I replied.

"You can stay. My parents are gone for three months in Paris setting up a new firm," he begged.

"No. I have something important tonight," I demanded.

"Well maybe this will change your mind," he said.

Jack got up and walked inside. This is the part in my head where he came back with a cleaver, or a knife, or maybe even a gun, and he killed me. Instead, he came back with a snack tray. On it was powder, a rusty spoon, a needle, a lighter, and a shoelace.

"You sure you can't stay," Jack persuaded.

"I-," I began.

"Shhh," he leaned over and put his hand on my shoulder. I tensed up.

"Relax," he said.

He gently caressed my arm as he tied the string real tight, right below my elbow. I didn't want to do it, but I sat there anyways. I felt it rush into my system and go all the way up my arm. I could feel it go straight to my heart, with a sharp pain as it coursed through my veins. Then I was gone. The best high of my life.

I forgot everything, even my name. I forgot about Connor, Zach, my parents, that kid from the protest. I just sat back and let reality fade away.

Chapter 20
POV Connor

Alex and I were in the best spot ever. After the incident, we both stepped down. Equality wasn't about me, it was never about me; it was about everyone. I just wanted to give them the courage to find their voice, and they did. My job was done, and my new job was about to begin. I started a company writing notes to LGBTQ+ teens. A few words of encouragement to help those who felt lost or lonely. I wasn't making any profit, it was all free, so between working and that, I had no time.

I had a lot on my plate, worrying about Alex and making sure he was alright with his head, and trying to save money to buy a house. Having to work two double shifts, come home, write letters to all those kids, package them in envelopes, and send them out the next morning, I was exhausted. The only thing that made me feel good was Alex.

I loved when I would be sleeping and I'd roll over and feel the warmth of his body up against mine. How he'd mumble cute things in his sleep like "I love you baby." It reminded me of how lucky I was to have a guy like him. A guy I wanted to one day marry and spend the rest of my life with. It was just a matter of waiting for him to pop the question, which I had a feeling was coming soon.

Alex was distant for some time, really distant. I could tell he was lying about something, I just didn't know what. Then, one day, I was doing laundry and I found a number on a sticky note in his pocket, so I called it. It was a jewelry store, and an expensive one.

I called my best friend and told her all about how he got a ring, and how any day, he could just pop the question. I was impatient at first, I mean a couple weeks had gone by and nothing, and then it all clicked. He was waiting for our one year anniversary.

He wasn't gonna be home that night because he wouldn't have been able to contain his excitement and would be afraid he'd spill the secret. We had reservations at this beach side restaurant right by the water. I had the whole night planned out. I'd get up to go to the bathroom, or turn my head to look at something, and when I came back, he'd be down on one knee. Of course I'd say yes, and then we'd be on to the next chapter of our life together.

So, the night came, and I got all dressed up. I had on these beige loafers, with white dress pants, a black belt, a dark blue button up shirt with pink flamingos on it, and my favorite silver watch. The watch was my grandfathers. He wore it every day and never took it off. When he passed, it was given to me. I wore it so that he could be with me, because I knew that he would want me to be happy, and I know that he would have wanted to be there, had he been alive.

When I got there, Alex hadn't checked in, so I went over to our spot he reserved and ordered a drink. It was a coke and rum to get me started, and a bottle of champagne for later. I sat there for hours, waiting and waiting. The sad thing is, I knew what was going on. I knew he wasn't stuck in traffic, or running late, but I kept making excuses for him. I kept thinking that, maybe, it was all planned, that he was secretly planning a big party back at the house. So I left and went back home. I walked in the door acting all surprised but no one was there. I don't know why I was hurt, I knew there wasn't going to be a big party. I knew Alex was out there somewhere, right at those moments, doing god knows what, leaving me all alone, so I called him.

"Hello?" Alex answered.

He was drunk, I could tell. His words were all sluggish, and he sounded dead.

"Babe?" I said.

"Who's this?" he questioned.

"It's Connor," I replied.

"You! Don't call me again!" Alex yelled.

"Where are you? I'm coming to get you!" I demanded.

"Are you stupid? I said leave me alone!" he yelled again.

"You're drunk, you don't mean that. Just tell me where you are so I can come get you," I begged.

"I'm not drunk, I'm high," he responded.

"You're what! Who are you with?" I asked angrily.

"The guy I've been sleeping with," he blurted out.

"What?" I said, hurt.

"Look, Alex doesn't want to talk to you, so don't call him anymore," an unknown voice said.

Just like that, he was gone. I sat there for a good fifteen minutes, just in shock of what had happened. Then came the anger. I texted him, and called him, but my number was blocked on his phone. I just wanted to scream at him. Why? Why do this? Why make me care when he knew he didn't? Why not have the guts to say it to my face? Why leave me, when all I'd done was help him? What did I do wrong to drive him away?

So many questions, and anger, and emotions. I didn't know what to do, so I went on a binge. My first reaction was to get drunk, so without thinking, that's what I did. I went to the liquor cabinet, skipped the whole glass, and just started drinking from the bottle. My eyes were too filled with tears to even see what it was, all I know is that it helped me forget.

I was hysterically crying. I mean screaming, and yelling, and flipping out. I went crazy, destroying the whole apartment. I got a knife and stabbed his pillow a thousand times until the stuffing was everywhere. I got all his clothes from the dresser and threw them out the window, drawer and all. It made this huge crack as it splintered on the street. All of that time believing in love, and believing that the world had good people in it, all for nothing.

I just wanted to punch him. I wanted to punch him, and just keep hitting, and hitting, and hitting, because he literally took everything from me. In one phone call, I went from planning the rest of my future, to feeling my heart get ripped out of my chest. When I closed my eyes, all I could see was red and black spots. I had to find him.

So, I stumbled downstairs and fell onto the street. I just laid there for a second, looking up at the moon and the stars. I saw a glimpse of a flashback to one of our first dates at the beach. I remember looking up at those stars, then over at him, and seeing his bright smile, and feeling hope and warmth. Now that smile brought me anguish and pain.

I jumped up, pants stained, shirt ripped, one shoe, and walked all the way down the street to my car and started it. I banged the dashboard and the steering wheel, and in the process, started to stomp my feet. I hit the gas pedal and flew forward, hitting the lamppost in front of me. I jumped out to see the front of my car smashed, but all I could do was laugh. Laugh as I got back into the car and drove down the street onto the highway.

I don't remember much of it, but they told me I lost control of the car and went off the overpass. I did two flips while falling, and then landed on the road below me, completely crossing the other side of the highway before hitting the median and stopping.

I remember thinking, while the car was doing the first flip, 'was it worth it Alex?' I remember being totally okay with it all, but having regret at the same time. Then I blacked out.

I was in and out of consciousness. I vaguely remember waking up, hanging upside down, still buckled into the seat of the car. I remember feeling my head wet, but it wasn't water. It felt sticky as it dripped down the side of my face. Then I saw a pair of headlights, and the sound of a car screeching as it came to a halting stop. I could hear the car doors open and close as someone came rushing towards me while on the phone with the police.

He was right next to me, but it sounded so distant. "Help! I need help! There was an accident!"

My eyes got really heavy, and I couldn't hold them open anymore, so I closed them. I felt an instant relief as I drifted away. I was sure I was dead. I saw my life flash before my eyes. All the happy memories with Alex: the laughs, the smiles, the cute dates. All of it. I was watching my past self, so happy, and I felt myself feeling it. I relived some of my best memories before crashing and falling. I don't know how to explain it, but suddenly, all the lively memories just turned grey, and everything felt sluggish, almost like time was being slowed down.

I was back at our apartment, sitting on the swivel stool at the kitchen island when I noticed a faint crack in the walls of the apartment. Then it started growing bigger and bigger until the wall collapsed. Behind it was this giant black hole sucking everything up: the furniture, the TV, even the couch. I was holding onto the kitchen counter when it finally took me in as well. As I screamed, a hand reached out and grabbed me, so I grabbed it back. I looked up to see the face of the person who had my life in their hands. It was Alex, and with the evilest of smiles, he just let go, watching and smiling as I fell to my death into the dark hole.

Next thing I knew, I was jumping up from what felt like the longest nap ever. I was sweating and I didn't know where I was. I tried to move my hand, but it was handcuffed down to the bed. I started pulling and panicking, and all these monitors started beeping and buzzing. "Calm down, relax! You're alright" a nurse said.

Chapter 21
POV Alex

I spent the next two months just strung out on Jack's couch, and not gonna lie, it felt amazing. It felt amazing to wake up, get high, sleep with Jack, and just waste all my time doing nothing.

I was reminded of why I used to get high in the first place, and forgot why I gave it up. I was blinded by all the lying and pain it was causing me. I didn't see all the problems it had brought into my life because I was in love with the temporary pain relief. My mind had been running for what felt like ever, and I was exhausted.

Years of always over thinking and being stressed thinking, 'I wish I was normal.' Always shutting out anyone who got remotely close to me because I had convinced myself that I was so annoying and so worthless that I didn't matter. I told myself that nobody would ever look at me and think 'I want to get to know him.' I didn't think anyone would ever want to love me.

Even when things were at their best with Connor, I still had that thought in the back of my mind, and it ate me alive. It was killing me to always overthink everything. My depression made all the good things feel bad, and my anxiety made all the bad things feel worse. Being numb was the only way I knew how to fix it. I began to depend on drugs just to be able to get out of bed in the morning. Being high just had this grasp on me that I couldn't escape. There were many days where I wanted to try and stay sober, but I just couldn't.

Ever day started out the same way, we'd make out and have sex. Just sex. Not like sex with love and passion, just sex. Meaningless sex, and I'm not going to lie, it wasn't good at all. In the beginning it was, because Jack was amazing, but being high was like having it all, and nothing could top that. Nothing could feel better than being high.

I'd go days without eating or drinking, and sometimes I would get so sick and nauseous that I'd feel like I was going to vomit, but there was nothing in my stomach but bile. I was so dehydrated that my skin lost all of it's color, and I remember sitting there feeling trapped. I wanted to do better so badly but I just didn't have it in me. It was so much easier to just sit there and rot away than to even try and fight. I was at rock bottom, and I really didn't think I was getting out. I should have tried harder, and looking back I'm mad at myself for giving in so easily because I know I had so much more fight left in me, but at the time I couldn't see it.

I hated being alive and feeling like that, because it was traumatizing. Even though the stuff happened years ago, It was as if I was reliving it everyday. When I woke up, it was the first thing on my mind. Whenever I was happy, I convinced myself I shouldn't have been. I told myself that, because I was fat, ugly, and the 'gay disappointment,' that

I could never be happy until I wasn't any of those things.

I couldn't change any of it, it was all still there, no matter how hard I tried. Those words were all embedded in my brain. I couldn't unhear them. All the times I walked into a room and everyone laughed. All the times I sat there like a fool, laughing with the people who were demeaning me. All the times I was told to kill myself, called: freak, ugly, fat, pig, weird, faggot, fag, sissy, useless, disgusting. The list never ended.

When I met Connor, some of it went away, but it was all still there for the most part, and I suppressed it. I shouldn't have started dating Connor, if I'm being honest, because I wasn't ready. I had so much work to do on myself, that I had no time to worry about Connor and his needs, but I was in love, and I put him before myself. I spent so much time worrying about him, making sure he was okay, and doing what I felt needed to be done to make him happy. In that whole process, I neglected myself, and more and more each day I drifted into the dark abyss that I like to call depression.

It took a whole year, but I was in the deep

end, and I was drowning. Drowning in pain, and I couldn't just bottle it all up and ignore it. I had to let it out, and drugs were the option. I was past getting help from a doctor. I was in this extreme self destructive phase and I didn't care who or what I hurt. I just wanted to feel okay.

I wasn't really doing that much damage. Besides Connor, I hadn't really hurt anyone. I spent my days in outer space, laying on some rich guy's couch while he enjoyed the company of another man. He was so far in the closet, he probably had just as much, if not more, problems to deal with than I did.

We belonged together. We could talk and say whatever we wanted, and neither of us would even remember it when we were sober. I loved every moment of it, even if it was my rock bottom, it felt amazing. Rock bottom felt so great, because, for the first time in a while, I could just close my eyes and not be there. I could close my eyes and not see Zach's face, or see that stupid classroom where he shoved me up against the lockers and hit me. Or see my mother's face when I came out to her, or feel the loneliness of not knowing what being happy felt like. It was all just gone. I had found the perfect way to cope with it all. I found the balance between being alive but feeling like I was dead.

Chapter 22
POV Jack

Growing up, I had a rough life. Yes it was an expensive luxurious life, but it was still rough. Just because we had money, and I was spoiled rotten, didn't make it the best childhood. I was the only son of two CEO's, and no matter how much they gave me, nothing could make up for all the things they missed. The two week vacations we'd go on, just so they could spend the whole time on the phone talking business. All the toys they bought me, just to keep me out of their hair so they could work. They thought that they could just throw money at all their problems in life, and for the most part it worked, except for me. I was the only problem that money couldn't fix.

I was a kid, what was I supposed to do? I made messes. I needed help and guidance along the way, but they were never there. To this day, I don't really know my parents. I just know that they're the type of people to put work before everything else. They never showed up to school plays, or parent teacher nights. It was solely about work.

I landed the lead role in our school play my sophomore year of high school. I was excited. I had been practicing for weeks. It was all I talked about. When I got home, I ran through the front doors, all the way up to my moms office. I burst through the doors shouting, "I made it! I made the part!" I was expecting my mother to be happy for me, but she just gave me this look of total confusion.

"What part?" my mother asked.

"I got the lead role!" I exclaimed.

"Oh, well can you make sure you shut the door on the way out," she replied, completely ignoring the great news I just told her.

She didn't even try to fake a smile or anything. She brushed off something I'd worked really hard on, something important to me she didn't care about because like always her work came first.

I never understood how anyone could enjoy all that money at the expense of losing everything else they owned. I mean yeah, we had three pools, and a yacht, but we never used any of it.

I always did, because I had nothing but time on my hands. However, my parents, all they did was work. Work so hard for things that they'd never get to enjoy. Lavish items that would just become dust collectors.

My dad left his house at fifteen and traveled across the country working on farms. He hadn't had any contact with his family in years. My mom was ten when her mother and father died in a car crash, resulting in her older sister taking her in. Her older sister, my Aunt Mary, was an evil woman. She always resented my mother because she felt my mother ruined her life. I mean, there she was, twenty two years old now having to raise a ten year old. I don't blame her for being angry, but she didn't have to treat my mother the way she did. She was an awful woman, and because of it, when my mom turned eighteen, she ran away and met my dad. That's when they started the business, and from there, somehow, they got to where they are now.

My point was that my parents didn't know what the word family meant, and I always thought that's what they were missing the most in life. So, I practiced, and practiced, until I had the whole script memorized. I put my all into it, making sure everything was perfect. I had them both promise they'd take off for opening night, and was so excited. In my eyes, that was the saving grace. They'd see what a family should be like, and realize what they were missing out on all these years. For the first time in their lives, they'd feel proud of me, and they'd maybe, just maybe, want to get to know me. As sad as it is, my parents had no idea who their own son was.

I had the whole night figured out, I'd walk out on the stage, see their smiles, and at the end, they'd clap and cheer, "that's my son!" We'd go out to dinner and we'd talk, not about work, but about the simple stuff. Maybe, that was a big maybe, if the night was going well, I'd finally talk to them about my sexuality.

I hadn't told them I was gay yet, and I was afraid. I was afraid because we didn't really talk enough for me to know how they stood on the subject of sexuality. I didn't know if they'd care or not, so I always tried to avoid telling them. However, I was dating this really cute guy named Liam, and I loved him. I loved him and I wanted to show him off and not hide him. My parents had no idea who their own son was, and it bothered me. I felt like I was deceiving them. I was hoping that night would be the beginning of our relationship as a healthy normal family.

Except, when I walked out on the stage shouting my first lines, I glanced over to the front row seats I'd reserved for them, and they were empty. I was so shook, I stuttered and messed up the easiest part of the whole play. I don't know how I did it, but I managed to get my act together, both literally and physically to get on with the show. After that, I went off stage while everyone on the crew was high-fiving and celebrating. I went straight to change and look at my phone. I had one notification. A text from my mother.

"Hey sweetie. I know tonight was opening night, but something happened and we had to go away for a couple days. We'll be home soon, stay safe."

I didn't even have the courage to respond. I changed into my regular clothes and called a taxi. On the way in the taxi, I had this middle aged man for a driver. We weren't talking much so I had a lot of time to think. To think about my parents, and how much my life sucked. I just wished I could change it all, and I didn't know how. I was craving attention, from all the years of neglect and being ignored. So, I did what any attention seeking teen does. I decided I'd throw a party.

I had this big mansion all to myself, so I might as well have gotten some use out of it. I invited some people, and told them to invite their friends. It kind of just snowballed down to a whole bunch of strangers all crowded into my house. I didn't really know any of them, I mean, I'd seen their faces in school, but none of them had ever talked to me before.

I remember being so confused about it all. There I was, surrounded by all these people, yet I'd never felt so alone in my life. Just watching all these people be so happy and normal. No pouting faces, or shy shadows lurking in the corner. Everyone was just so happy and carefree. I was getting so mad that I had to leave. I ran away into my room and lost it. I flipped my mattress and just kept swinging and swinging. I knocked over shelves and I threw stuff. I was just tired.

I prayed I could let go just for once, but I never could find the courage to do it. I always hesitated, or held back, and seeing those people, I don't know, it just made me mad. How, to most people, being goofy and embracing themselves came naturally, but to me, I had to fight for it. It made me frustrated, because my whole life, I had always been playing the role of what others wanted me to be. I never truly knew how to be myself. I always had friends, but I had to fake it around them, and I was tired of keeping up that facade .

I wanted friends that got my humor and laughed at my jokes. I wanted friends that I didn't have to be embarrassed to talk about myself in front of. Who would laugh with me, instead of laughing at me. I wanted to surround myself with people who understood me and encouraged me to be passionate about things, rather than brush off the things I felt were important. I never had that, and I felt I deserved it.

I closed my eyes and kept swinging until my arm felt like it was going to fall off. Then, I just fell to the ground. I put my hand to my face and it was wet. When I looked down, there was shattered glass everywhere, and the palms of my hand had tiny cuts all across it. I sat there, blood dripping down my hands onto my pants, sighed and got up to go wash them out.

I walked into the bathroom, and laying in the tub was Samantha. This short, skinny, flat chested girl, with the curliest hair I had ever seen. She had no fashion sense whatsoever. It was very basic: ripped jeans, a crop top, a scrunchie on her wrist, a vape in one hand, and a beer in the other. She had platinum blonde hair and the most horrendous of fake spray tans I'd ever seen. Sitting on the toilet next to her was Josh. Josh was hot, if I'm being totally honest, but he was also straight. He had curly brown hair cut kind of short on the sides with a little bit of length on top. He was somewhat built, but for the most part, he was just skinny. He was the kid who, if he inhaled deep enough, you could see his rib cage.

They were startled at first when I came in. Samantha jumped up screaming, and Josh ran to come help me, but I was fine. It looked worse than it felt.

"Are you okay dude?" Josh asked me.

"Yeah, I'm fine, it's nothing," I said nonchalantly.

"That looks bad, what happened?" Samantha questioned.

"Nothing," I hesitated.

I didn't feel like explaining it all to them, so I figured I'd just let their imagination run wild, and whatever they thought, they thought. I didn't care much about my public reputation. If people thought I was a bad-ass who got into a fight, or a nut case with anger issues, what did it matter? My parents didn't care about me, I didn't care about me, so why in the world would I care what other people thought?

"Do you want to go to the hospital? 'Cause you're bleeding a lot," Josh asked.

"It's all good. I'll handle it," I brushed him off.

The two of them walked out, and I shut the door behind them, locking it. I turned on the water, as cold as it could go, and ran my hands under it. It stung and burned, but it wasn't an extreme pain. The water and blood mixed together, washing out the cut, and stained the white sink a tint of red. I was there for about ten minutes, just looking at my reflection in the mirror, waiting for the blood to stop.

I remember looking at myself and thinking what a disappointment I was, not just to myself, but to everyone. How I had so much potential to be this amazing person, but I blew it. Instead of doing things right, and being normal, I was just different, and I didn't think it would ever change.

Most seniors in high school look forward to taking the perfect girl to the prom. They look forward to buying a tuxedo, and admiring their beautiful date in a stunning gown, all made up with their makeup and nails done. The perfect set of heels to match the whole outfit, and a corsage on her wrist. It sounds perfect, but not for me.

I wanted to be the girl, not physically, but I wanted to be the one admired. The one in the heels and the dress. My whole life I've had this feminine side I'd repressed for so long, and the more I pushed it down, the more it bubbled up. It's why I was so angry with life, and why I could never be myself. I didn't want to wear jeans and polo shirts. I wanted to have my nails done and wear crop tops. I was miserable, because everyday I had to get up and be someone I hated. How could anyone be happy living like that? The more I looked in the mirror, the more I got disgusted with who I was because it wasn't me.

When I was little, maybe about eleven or twelve, I used to spend a lot of time over at this nanny's house. This was when I was too young to care for myself, so my parents had no choice but to pay someone else to raise me rather than take a day off. In all honesty though, I'll never really complain about my time spent there. I don't know her full name because I only referred to her as Ms. Mandy, but she was this sweet old lady, and I had a lot of fun with her. She was a shopaholic. She had two whole walls with shelves put on them to show off her heels. In the living room closet, she had all her fur coats from when she was younger. She even had a whole wardrobe closet in the garage for all her gowns and dresses. We used to go through them every once and awhile. One time we counted, she had over a hundred pairs of shoes. It was more than she'd ever used, and most of the stuff had barely even been worn.

When I went there, she'd always be cleaning, or doing something. So, for the most part, I didn't really have much supervision. I mean, she was there, but she wasn't exactly paying attention to me. I used to make a peanut butter sandwich with the crunchy peanut butter, and sit down in the living room watching cartoons for hours. One day, I must have seen the same episode a thousand times, so I shut the TV off and sat there in frustration and boredom. I remember checking the clock every two seconds to see if it was five o'clock and my mom was on her way. Time felt like it was going so slow, I didn't think it would ever come.

I got to a point where I was so bored that I did what any young child does when they're bored; I decided to look around for something to do. I went through the junk drawer, looking for a deck of cards to play solitaire, but there weren't any. I saw Ms. Mandy from the kitchen window across the street talking to the neighbor, and I decided to take the time to go look through her stuff. She had this chest in her room that she always told me not to go in. She said it was her personal stuff. That only meant one thing to me, which was I had to see what was in there. I expected it to be like stacks of money, or maybe like something crazy she was hiding. So, I walked over and into the room, shutting the door behind me. I walked over to the chest at the foot of her bed, took off the two folded blankets she kept on top, and lifted it up. It was so old that it made the loudest creaking noise I'd ever heard. I honestly thought I broke it. On the inside was nothing but closed envelopes.

I started planning my whole shopping list of

what I was gonna do with all the cash. I was gonna get a new TV, a new phone, a remote control car, and a new bike. I could almost feel the wind brushing up against my face as I pedaled down the street on a summer night with all my friends, but my dream was crushed rather quickly when I realized that instead of stacks of hundreds, it was all just old photos.

I was so disappointed. What was the big fuss about? She didn't want me seeing her photos? I mean you could barely see the outline of the people in them, they were so old. All torn and ripped in black and white with no color. I was so annoyed, it was all such a deceitful story. I really thought she had gold or something hidden in there. Then, I found it.

A small drawstring bag that was tied with a double knot to keep whatever inside extra secure. The smile came back to my face and I felt the blood rush from my feet to my head. I was so excited, this was the big surprise, and a surprise it was. Inside were all her expensive jewelry. Her diamond engagement ring, her pearls, and a gold chain. I'd never really seen jewelry like that before, it was all so expensive. You could tell just by looking at it that it was real.

I remember how appealing the engagement ring was to was to me. Just looking at it made me happy. I held it for about ten minutes before I decided to slip it onto my finger. It was incredibly big and kept slipping off, but I felt so different with it on. I felt like I had discovered a new power from that ring. I loved how it looked on me, and how it felt on my fingers. I was so caught up in the moment that I decided I'd give myself a whole makeover.

I put on this bracelet, and a ring on each finger, with a big necklace that practically went all the way down to my belly button. I looked into the mirror, and I looked so ridiculous, but I felt empowered. I then walked over to the closet and pulled out a pair of these blue high heels. The minute my toe went into those shoes, I changed. I wasn't insecure or shy, I wasn't afraid anymore. It gave me confidence, I don't know how else to explain it, but it made me feel like I was on top of the world. I fell in love with all of them. The way I walked in the heels, the way the bracelets dangled when I moved my arm. The visual appeal of looking at myself and seeing who I truly was.

I went from dreading going to that awful house to practically begging to go there every chance I could. I would sit from the living room, watch my parents pull out of the driveway, and sit on the couch until Ms. Mandy would get distracted with something. Whether it be cooking or cleaning, once I was sure she wouldn't know I was gone, I'd sneak off. I'd grab a different pair of shoes each time and put together my own outfit. I'd make believe I was in the real world like that. I would pretend to be a doctor, or a lawyer. I'd have an old folder I found filled with bills and unimportant papers that she had sitting in a bag in one of her drawers, and I would act like I was in a real office.

It's crazy to explain it, but those clothes really gave me power. I could feel so puny and insecure, but the second I put on that 'outfit' I felt so different. I had the courage to be president if I wanted to. Nothing could have stopped me when I was wearing a pair of heels. That is until my father found out about my secret. You see, I used to be really cautious about making sure I had everything back to normal and was changed before my parents pulled up, but one day, I guess I lost track of time and they came to get me. My dad walked in the house and I didn't hear the doorbell or anything. I just heard approaching footsteps, and before I could even get to lock the door, he walked in. It was an awkward silence as he saw his son in heels, with jewelry, and he laughed, so I laughed too.

I was rather surprised by his reaction, and I thought it was all too good to be true. I guess I was right, because that night, when I was laying in bed, he came over to my room and sat at the edge of my bed to 'talk' to me. I already knew what he was gonna say because my father never talked to me, but I acted like I didn't know what was up, and I let him talk.

"Son, we need to talk about earlier. I know it was a joke, and that was very funny, but you can't do that. If the other kids at school find out, they'll make fun of you. Boys don't wear clothes like that, it's not normal, and you're my son, not my daughter," he said.

That was it, that was the conversation he had with me, not even a hug goodnight, he just left. I wasn't even old enough to completely understand my sexuality, I just knew I liked those types of things, and I didn't understand why it was a big deal. Why couldn't a guy paint his nails, or wear high heeled shoes, because only girls did that kind of stuff. I thought how unfair it all was, and I agreed to save myself the trouble of getting yelled at. I'd never wear that stuff again.

Looking at myself in the mirror that night of the party, I felt my stomach turn inside out because none of it was me. Those clothes, the short hair, just everything about myself. I hated it all and I wanted to change. I wanted to feel like I belonged, so I pulled myself together and wrapped the hand towel across my palm and walked out those doors. I was ready to burst out into tears, but I somehow found it in me to walk with such confidence, even though I wanted to crawl under a table and hide.

I could only describe my walk as cocky. I felt like I was the scum of the Earth, but found it in me to walk like a king. Smiling and talking to people like it was nothing. I guess acting was just something I became good at. My whole life has been an act, so I guess I just got used to being dead on the inside and managing to smile and act like life was good.

I took about fifteen steps before I felt the tears and the frown pushing their way through the smile. I felt a surge of sadness coming over me like water from a dam, and I knew this time I couldn't pull off the act. I didn't know what to do, so I ran over to the liquor table and poured myself a glass of Vodka. I poured half a glass and started to drink it. I thought it would be like in the movies where they swallow it and it tastes a little bitter and I'd make a face of disgust, but I was wrong. Instead, it was like tasting pure rubbing alcohol, the first drop that hit my tongue burnt like battery acid. I started coughing and choking, and who do you think came running over to me? None other than Samantha and Josh from earlier.

The two of them we're laughing at my little accident. I felt crappy before, but now at that point, I was beyond embarrassed. I stood there, red in the face while they laughed at me.

"Oh, don't be ashamed. We all have an embarrassing first time story," Samantha said.

"The first time I smoked weed, I got so messed up that i stripped down to my underwear and everyone got a video of me twerking," Josh said.

"I once thought it would be a good idea to drink cheap wine on an empty stomach and threw up so bad I bruised my esophagus" Samantha laughed.

"Really?" I questioned.

"Yeah! We all gotta learn at some point," she smiled.

"What do you say we leave here and go to a club to get you some good stuff?" Josh asked.

I didn't know what to say, so I just went along with it, which was a mistake because I wasn't in a rational state of mind. I just wanted to fit in, and they were the first two people to show interest in me in a while. I was afraid to say no and blow it, so I left with them.

We got in their car and drove about twenty minutes into the city to this club. They were talking a lot, but I was kind of silent. I didn't really know what to say, and I didn't want to say something stupid, so I didn't talk. I felt so out of place because I didn't belong there. Little did I know, that night was when I'd change. The night I'd go from the honor roll student who never broke any rules, to the rebel addict who now despised the idea of listening to anyone other than himself.

We were in this long line for the club and everyone there was visibly older than us. I was wondering what trick Samantha and Josh had up their sleeve to get us in there. As the line got closer and closer, they didn't fill me in on anything and I began to panic. I sat there sweating, my heart pounding as it went from ten people, to five, and then there we were, next in line. These two big bodyguards were standing in front of the doors. They had on all black suits with big sunglasses and the wire in their ears. In front of us were these two obnoxious drunk girls. They kept bumping into us and were yelling the whole wait. They walked over to the two emotionless giants who opened the door to let them in. From inside, I could see the flashing lights, a mosh-pit of people, and for a brief second, I heard some music and then the door shut. We were next.

"ID please," the bouncer said.

ID? I didn't have an ID. I was sure Josh or Samantha had some plan, but they just reached into their pockets and pulled out fake one's. They looked at me, and I guess they could tell by the terror and fear in my eyes I didn't have one, so they just ditched me. They walked inside and the door shut behind them. I didn't know what to do. I kind of just stood there for a second before I heard some angry mumbles behind me and figured I'd better leave and stop testing my luck.

I walked aimlessly around the city for hours with no purpose. I'm not going to lie, it was kind of soothing and calm. Being by myself was fun because I couldn't disappoint anyone anymore. I could be who I wanted to be and nobody I cared about would know or say anything. I mean, sure, I might have gotten the occasional dirty look or mumble, but it didn't matter.

I had been walking for about an hour and a half until I stopped at this Asian place that looked super cool on the outside. It had giant LED neon signs covering the whole front window in cool designs and shapes. It definitely stood out from all the other places and triggered my curiosity. So I figured I'd stop in, I mean what else did I have to do with my time?

The inside of the place was crazy insane, there was nobody else in there but this young couple in the far back corner that were sharing a plate of sushi. There were giant tanks everywhere filled with these exotic fish that were sorts of vibrant colors. I found this one stingray that caught my eye, he was significantly smaller than all the others, but he was cute. I walked over to the counter and I ordered a hibachi dinner and sat at a table all by myself. When the guy came to give me the check it came to twenty-five dollars, and I only hundred dollar bills in my wallet, so I just left that in the little tiny black booklet with the receipt. I was expecting to feel a little bit better after doing all that, but I still felt empty inside.

From there, I wandered around for a bit before I found this thrift shop. I was walking by when I saw a pair of shoes sitting on the display in the window; red bottomed high heel stilettos. I'd always wanted a pair, but never had the courage to buy them. I felt a little risky that night, so I walked into the store and over to the display in the window. I paused for a second. Once I was sure nobody was looking, I grabbed them and then grabbed the nearest shirt to hide them under it so that nobody could see I had them in my hands. I don't know who I was expecting to see, it was Two O'clock on a Tuesday night, the only people in there were me and this young girl working the register. Nonetheless, I snuck over to the changing room and threw the shirt to the side. I sat down, unlaced my sneakers and slipped my foot into the heels. It was a perfect fit. I remember the smile on my face as I looked in the small mirror. The smile where your cheeks actually hurt, and I remember I couldn't stop either. I was just so happy, because for the first time in, I don't know how long, I felt like me again. I felt like I had taken the mask off and I could finally breathe.

After all that, I had to buy them. The girl working was very goth. She was wearing a short mini skirt with ripped fishnet stockings and platform boots. She had black hair with neon green bangs and she seemed really nice. I put the shoes on the counter and she smiled.

"Ah, these are really cute. I'm surprised nobody else has gotten them yet," she said.

"Thanks," I responded.

"She's gonna love them," the cashier said.

"She?" I asked.

"Your girlfriend," she replied.

"Ohhh, yeah," I answered.

I felt such an awkward tension between us as I handed her the money and waited for my change. I wanted to tell her they were for me, but at the same time I was scared and afraid, but before I could even process what I was in my head I just blurted it out.

"I don't know why I lied, they're actually for me," I said.

I prepared myself for the judgmental stare, or the scoff followed by a rude comment, but for once I was wrong.

"Oh my gosh, you're gonna look sooo good in those! Good for you!" the cashier exclaimed.

That was the first time someone ever complimented me like that. The first time someone encouraged me to be me. I didn't know what to say other than blush and stand there glued to the ground.

"Walking might be a little rough because they're higher than most shoes, but you'll adjust," she smiled.

I was so amazed by her kindness that I wanted to just hug her and make her know how much it really meant to me. Sometimes, it's the smallest of words that make the biggest impacts. "I'm proud of you," "I'm happy for you," "You look good." All simple words that could change your whole day. In the midst of it all, I also felt sick. Sick that I could find comfort in total strangers, but my own parents made me feel like dirt and dragged me down. But that night wasn't about my parents, it was about me. So, I put my new shoes on and stumbled my way out the front door and onto the street.

I could barely walk, and the whole height thing took a little bit of adjusting, but before I knew it, I was walking like I did any other day. I felt such confidence like I was a god or something. I was suddenly immune to it all, the staring, the comments, all of it seemed to be ineffective now. I was finally me, and it felt amazing.

I walked about three blocks until I passed a vendor selling those glow in the dark sunglasses, and I passed this overflowing clothing donation box with stuff all over the sidewalk. I intended on walking right by it before I saw the strap of a purse sticking out from one of the black garbage bags. I ripped it open, and inside was all old dirty clothes, stained yellow and brown, but on top was a gently used red purse. It was fate, it matched the shoes, and I'd always wanted a purse before, so I had to take it.

The more time passed, the more I realized the problem wasn't me, but my situation. I couldn't survive in an environment where I wasn't accepted. I had to be myself. It was time to take that leap of faith and let go. I was walking back towards the bus station to get home and was trying to figure out how I was going to tell my parents, when I somehow came across a drag show.

I was walking, unaware of what was even going on, when all of a sudden these Queen's came yelling at me, complimenting my shoes and insisting I let them give me a makeover. I didn't know what to do. I'll admit, I was scared at first, but once I got to know them, I realized they were all just people. Amazing, kind, uplifting people who just wanted to have fun and do what made them happy. They weren't any different than I was, and I felt bad for judging them at first.

There was one in particular who I really clicked with, Charmaine. She said I really reminded her of herself when she was my age, and we got to talking. A lot of the stuff I had to say she related to, and she gave me a lot of good advice and words of encouragement. It was amazing to talk to someone who wasn't straight and actually understood what I was going through. Someone who wouldn't just brush off my problems and tell me how to feel. Someone who empathized with me, rather than accuse me of overreacting.

All of them seemed so happy to help get me ready, and I'd never had anyone take that much interest in me. They were poking and prodding all over my face with brushes and makeup sponges. "Close your eyes," "Tilt your head up," "Look forward." I felt like a puppet.

They did go all out on me: wig, lipstick, eyelashes, and they even gave me a dress. When it was all said and done, they were all crowded around me, smiling and admiring how stunning I looked. That's when they handed me the mirror and I lost it.

"Don't cry, you'll mess up the makeup!" Charmaine said.

That was me. That was who I was supposed to be. I was, for the first time ever, truthfully honest with myself, and open with who I am. It made me cry because it was a level of happiness I could have never imagined. By that time in my life, I was so depressed that I didn't think I'd ever smile again. I was so used to acting like I cared, that I lost touch with what true happiness actually felt like. In those moments, I felt it all rush back: the adrenaline, my heart beating, the true me returning. The cheerful, joyful, positivity that I once had, came flowing back into me and I suddenly felt enjoyment in life. I felt like I really cared, and I no longer had to put effort into wanting to believe in a better future. I felt hope, and determination; feelings I thought were gone. It no longer hurt to think of a lifestyle where I was myself, because I was living my dream, and it felt everything like I had imagined.

I had so much courage and happiness that I left my friends early before the show started and took a bus back home. The whole bus ride I sat there thinking of how I'd tell my parents when they came back, and I was so sure they'd understand and want what was best for me. I rehearsed it a thousand times. I knew exactly what I'd say and how it would go. I was ready to finally be me; to finally be happy. And I knew that once they would see how happy I really was they'd accept me for it.

By the time the bus had came to by stop I was exhausted, and wanted to pass out. As I walked in the front doors I noticed the party had ended itself. And all I could think about was my bed, but the place was trashed. Empty cups, and bottles everywhere. Stuffed in the one couch cushion I found a wallet and a pair of keys. On the kitchen counter there was a black lace bra-let. I couldn't even begin to process dealing with the mess, but I knew I had to at least clean some of it up, so I kept the wig and the makeup on as I picked up all the junk that littered the floors. Three garbage bags later and the kitchen and living room where finally somewhat presentable. And just as I sat down on the couch ready to pass out from exhaustion, I heard a distant moan. I jumped up and ran over to the other side of the house where there was a girl. She was very drunk and could barely walk. In her hands was a small little baggy with coke in it. I'd never seen or done drugs before, so I just took it from her and put it in my pocket because I didn't trust her with it. I mean, she was very out of it, so I called her a ride and sent her home, without the drugs. After that, I crashed on the floor until late into the next day.

When I woke up, my wig was still on, but my makeup was smudged everywhere and stained on my arm. I took a really hot shower, and when I got out, I paused for a second. I could hear talking; my mom and dad. I froze. The night before I was gung-ho to tell them, but that was before they were in the other room. I wanted to tell them, but coming out is rough because you don't know.

You think you know, but you are never sure. In a perfect world, it shouldn't matter if you're straight or not, but we don't live in a perfect world.

Coming out means opening yourself up to criticism and hate by people who will never understand you, but yet feel the need to judge you and your decision. It means sharing your deepest darkest secret that you've had to keep hidden for years, and now you're forcing yourself to tell everyone. It's like shining a giant spotlight on one of your biggest insecurities and knowing people are going to make fun of and mock you for it. The hardest part is not knowing the reactions of the people you're going to tell. You may think they'll support you, but in reality, they turn out to hate you, or vice versa.

I had so many thoughts going through my head that I began to get sick from it. The room started spinning, I felt my throat closing, and my face getting red. I didn't know what to do or say. I was afraid to come out, but I couldn't go back to the way things were. I made the hardest decision of my life that day, and I decided I had to do it. I got dressed, went into the living room, sat my parents down and told them. It took some leading up to, and I started to choke up, but then I just blurted it out, "I'm gay."

As kids, we want to believe our parents want what's best for us. I mean, they're the only reason we exist. They made a conscious decision all those years ago to have a kid. Part of that decision was to love and accept that kid throughout the rest of their lives. To be there for us when we're sick, help us with math homework, teach us how to ride a bike and tie our shoes. From the very beginning, we've always depended on them. Even when we're grown and we can fend for ourselves, we still need them to teach us all the important life lessons along the way. We're wired to need our parents because they're our teachers in life. They teach us the important lessons, like how to have proper manners, and how to keep a good friendship.

I think it's every gay kids dream to have parents who don't care about their sexuality. Parents that would hug them and tell them, "I love you and support you and I'll always be proud of you." Even though I wanted that, I knew it wasn't going to happen, because those types of things are just rare in today's world. Most parents flip out at first, and than gradually overtime become more accepting to it. However, my parents were not like that at all. My mom cried and cried for two days straight. My dad wouldn't look me in the eye for about a week. Then, one day, I was coming home from school when I saw my mom sitting in the passenger seat of the car. She was crying as usual, and when I opened the door, I bumped straight into my dad.

"Get into the car son," my father said.

I didn't know what was going on, but I knew it was bad. I didn't even get a chance to go inside. He just pushed me out of the way as he locked the doors with his key. I stood there zoning out, and then I heard the sound of the car honking as my dad waved for me to get in. I had a gut feeling something was going on, and I should have listened to it.

We drove for hours on this one lane road that was in the middle of two corn fields. The corn stalks were so tall that you couldn't see anything on either side of the car. From the backseat, all I could see out of the front window was an endless road. Twice my dad had to pull over so that the oncoming cars could pass; that's how narrow the road was. They were college kids, and they must have been off-roading because their trucks were all covered in mud. Other than that, there weren't any other signs of people for miles.

I started to get that eerie feeling that someone could kill us on that road and no one would know. We had no cell service, and I'm not even sure if electricity existed this far out. It seemed like we had left Earth and gone to a new planet where people didn't exist. We drove past a couple houses, but they were all abandoned. There was an old farm with a big giant empty silo that was spray painted with graffiti all up the side. Next to it was an old brick house that had one wall, which had completely given in and collapsed on the rest of the house, and then the barn. The paint had been stripped off almost entirely from being weathered down, and several pieces of wood were missing including the front doors.

After what seemed like forever, my father slowed down to make the turn onto this little dirt path that was paved between the corn fields. It was very narrow, and our side mirrors kept hitting the stalks next to us, and then it just opened up. In front of us, we were looking at what looked like an old Georgian estate. Three floors high, with two big double doors made of solid oak, a wrap-around porch, those giant pillars, and two rocking chairs with an older couple sitting there drinking what looked like coffee.

The man, his name was Rich, had a big long beard down to his stomach with long knotted hair that looked like it hadn't been washed in weeks. His wife Meredith, had barely any teeth in her mouth, and this frizzy brown mullet. They just sat there eyeing us as we pulled up to their house. I assumed my dad had made a wrong turn or something and I was waiting for him to change the gear into reverse, but instead, he parked it. Him and my mother got out.

I don't know how I knew, but I knew what was happening. Nobody had to say anything, I could just tell that this was it. They were dropping me off to get 'fixed.' This was their sick twisted way of making me straight. I jumped up, reaching over the center console and to the drivers side door pressing the lock button so they couldn't get in, but what use did I have, I couldn't escape this one. So, I sat there, heart racing, sweat dripping down my face watching my mom search through her bag for the key's while my dad yelled at me to open the doors from outside the car. I prayed so hard to god that she wouldn't find them, but she did. As soon as I saw her lift up her hand and heard the click, I just went numb. This was it.

My dad opened the door and I kicked him square in the face sending him flying back and into the dirt creating a cloud of dust. My mother started screaming at me, but I didn't care, he was dead to me. My panic turned into anger and I started to run, to the old barn we passed or to maybe find a gas station, I don't know where, but I wasn't staying there. I'd rather have starved in the woods than stay there.

As I ran, I felt my heart pumping faster and faster until it was going to explode, yet I kept pushing myself. I told myself I couldn't give up, and no matter what, I couldn't look back. I just had to run. I don't know what I was thinking, because eventually, I got so tired that I just collapsed to the ground. Laying there on my back, panting as I looked up at the sky. It was starting to get dark and the sky was that mix of light blue and orange. I had given up at that point, my brain was telling me to get up and run, but my legs wouldn't budge.

Before I knew it, these two big husky men came and picked me up. I was lifeless, and I didn't fight back. I just laid there as one of them grabbed my legs, and the other my arms. Together, the two men swung my limp body into the back of their truck and drove off. I let go and gave up total control. With each bump we went over, my head bounced back and forth. I was so exhausted I couldn't even try to fight. Not a physical exhaustion, but a mental exhaustion. I was so emotionally tired, I just wished I could shut off my brain and not feel anything. I wished for one second to not have to deal with my thoughts.

Dealing with depression and anxiety is hard because it doesn't just go away, and the more you ignore it, the worse it gets. The only way to really fix it is to get help, and that's scary. It's scary to tell your parents or an adult that you need to see a therapist or a doctor because you're afraid of being labeled as something you're not. You don't want to be seen like all the stereotypes, and then suddenly everyone is viewing you differently, when in reality you're still the same exact person. People start checking in on you, and not because they care enough to actually ask those questions, but god forbid something happened, they'd feel too guilty with themselves if they didn't. You can't be sad or angry without it being over proportionalized and seen as manic. I mean, we wonder why people are afraid to talk about suicide and these other problems, it's because talking about it in most cases makes it worse. People try to make us feel guilty by saying 'think of all the people you'd hurt,' or 'you're being selfish.' For me, taking my life would have been a selfless act, because believe me, I wanted to live, I really wanted to live, but I felt like no matter what I did, I would always be a let down. In my own way, killing myself would have been an apology to my parents. As twisted as it sounds, I didn't know what else I could do. I was sorry I was gay and feminine, and all the other flaws they saw in me, but that was me, and I didn't know how to change. Taking my life was the only answer I saw.

In a split second, without thinking, I leaned over towards the door, put all my weight on it, and pulled the handle out. The door opened slightly, and from all the pressure of my body weight, it swung open entirely, and out I went. I hit the dirt and did several barrel rolls until I came to a stop. I wasn't dead, but I was hurt, and mad. Mad because I really wanted it all to end. The depression was too exhausting, it was debilitating. Every time I tried to be happy, my mind would start wandering, and I'd go into this trance-like state. All the thoughts would come flooding in, "You aren't good enough," "You can't be happy," "You don't deserve this," "You suck," "You're a terrible person." Then I'd get lost in it all, and I'd miss out on everything. While everyone else was laughing, I was having a mental breakdown as all my emotions mixed and churned in my head. Anger, sadness, anxiety, scared, miserable, all of them so intense. I felt like I needed to scream and cry, but I could never bring myself up to it. I was ready to explode, and I guess I did.

When they reversed the truck and got out to get me back in, my fight or flight instincts kicked in. I wanted to die, but not like that. You see, I had so much hope, but no reinforcement for it. I wanted so badly to be positive, but how could I? Nothing good ever happened to me, it was just one bad thing followed by another. I wanted to live, but not like that. I wanted to be happy, and fall in love. I wanted to go on cute dates, sing songs, and smile. I didn't want to always feel guilty, or depressed. I was exhausted from dealing with the burden of constantly walking around spending every minute reminding myself of what a failure I was. I was just so tired of feeling bad about who I was, that I wanted to run away. I wanted to run away from it all, and I did, but I still managed to fail.

They came back and got out of the truck like before, except this time, they were much more aggressive. The bigger one put his knee right in the center of my back and pinned me down to the ground. I was paralyzed as sharp pains shot up and down my spine simultaneously in both directions. I could see the other one out of the corner of my eye as he helped lift me up and tie my hands together. It was useless to even try to fight, so I hoped that maybe my parents would see me all tied up and have a change of heart, but when I got back, they were gone. In those moments, my heart sank. This was really it, this was the end.

"Your folks left. I sent 'em home. I promised them I'd take good care of ya. Why don't you go inside and get acquainted with the other fellas," the guy Rich said.

He nodded his head as if to signal to the two men to bring me inside, so they did as they were told. It was very old fashioned: the furniture, the wallpaper, the appliances, even the smell. There was a big giant room that was split between a living room and a dining room. The living room had a sofa, and a love-seat that had the ugliest floral print on it I'd ever seen. It was covered in those plastic covers that made the crinkling noises every time you moved. The TV didn't work, it was only there for show, if you tried to turn it on, all you got was static. They said the only thing we needed to focus on was our recovery, and the TV would "distract us from our goal of getting better." The dining room had this long solid oak table with a big centerpiece in the middle on a white lace runner that went down the whole middle of the table. The chairs were very heavy, and you had to lift them up to sit down because they wouldn't slide. There was also a curio that was filled with old china in it that was only there for decoration. I was told it came from Meredith's grandparents.

I didn't see the upstairs because we weren't allowed up there. I was brought through the kitchen to this little tiny locked door that looked like a pantry. Except, on the other side were stairs that led to the basement. It was very steep and each step I took was followed by a loud creek. At the bottom were about twelve mattresses all on the floor. That was it. The whole basement was empty except for twelve paper thin flat mattresses with no pillows or blankets. On each mattress laid a young boy about my age, except for one on the far left side. Nobody looked up when I came down, they all just laid there looking lifeless like zombies. I didn't expect them to jump for joy, but I would have thought they'd have some reaction, but it didn't even phase them.

The two guys didn't even tell me what mattress was mine; they just cut the ties on my hand and pushed me forward to the ground before going back up and locking me in. I got myself up on my feet and stood there for a second hoping that maybe, because the guys were gone, they'd be friendly, but still nothing. I finally realized that I wasn't dealing with a friendly crowd, and I went over to the empty spot. I laid down on my back, hands folded on my chest, and looked up at the boards above me in what I think was the kitchen.

"You alright?"

I turned to my right to see this short skinny kid with straight black hair turned to his side looking at me.

"I don't know," I said.

"My name's Jake," he told me.

"Jack," I replied.

"It seems scary at first, but you adjust. My first day I was scared out of my mind, and then one day, I just got used to it," Jake said.

"How long did that take you?" I asked.

"I don't know why I lied, I'm still not used to it, I don't think I ever will be," he said chuckling.

Jake and I became friends very quickly. I mean, at first, I was very quiet and I didn't talk to anyone just like the other kids. I went to 'therapy' and did what I had to to get the days over with. I had no idea if, or when, I'd even be able to go home, and it just felt like an endless time loop. Every day was the exact same; wake up at five for breakfast, group therapy from seven to eight, chores around the farm and the house, then lunch, then another hour of therapy, and finally some time to shower before eating dinner and going to bed. One of my favorite jobs to do out of all of them was tend to the horses. Something about their presence was soothing to me. I would sit there gently brushing their mains, and as crazy as it sounds, I'd talk to them. I knew they weren't listening, but every now and again I'd get a whimper or a neigh as if they could actually understand me. I know it sounds stupid, but that's what I had to tell myself to get through it all. It was a lot every day sitting through those classes being told how I was an abnormal freak and I needed to change. God forbid any of us ever spoke up, we'd get punished and sent into a locked closet. I myself had never seen it, but it must have been bad because every time Rich brought it up, everyone seemed to shutter. So, I just had to sit there and swallow it all.

Then one day things changed. I was out back feeding the horses, when I started to talk to them, like I normally do.

"I just don't understand what's so hard about it? Why can't people just accept us? I mean, why is being gay a bad thing? How is me kissing a guy bothering anyone? I didn't ask for it. I didn't ask for any of this. Do they think I asked to be different? That I asked to be seen as the family screw up? That I wanted to be bullied and feel like trash all the time? I'm sick of it! I wish I could just fix it all!" I ranted.

"You can," Jake chimed in.

"Oh. Uh, how long were you there?" I turned around and asked embarrassingly.

"Not long," he said.

"Sorry," I said.

"It's nothing I haven't thought of myself," Jake responded.

"Why is this happening to us?" I questioned.

"I don't know," he answered.

There was an awkward silence before either of us spoke. It was weird to talk about feelings like that. I'm sure all of us felt like that, but I mean nobody ever said it out loud. To be honest, I was embarrassed because I didn't want to be seen as this softy who couldn't take care of himself and got emotional, so I just brushed it all off.

"I'm just finishing up, then I'll meet you at the house," I said.

Chapter 23
POV Jake

I had been there about four months before Jack had arrived. I was sent there the day after I came out. It wasn't planned to go down the way it did, but I can't change the past. You see, I had no intentions of coming out. I knew my parents wouldn't accept me or love me for who I was so I kept it a secret. I dated girls, played sports; all the stuff they expected me to do. Then I met Luca. Luca was the love of my life.

We had a Spanish class together my junior year. It was love at first sight. I mean, he was attractive, but it was more than that. It was the way he smiled, the look in his eyes; everything about him made me almost melt on the inside. I didn't think I could love someone like that until I saw him.

At first, I didn't think we would ever work out. I was dating this girl. Her name was Candace and we were sort of serious. The two of us had been together for five months, and I didn't want to hurt her. Despite being gay, I had spent a considerable amount of time with her, and the last thing I wanted to do was hurt her feelings. I also didn't know if Luca felt that way about me, so I brushed it off, and told myself it wasn't meant to be. That whole day, despite telling myself to let it go, I couldn't stop thinking about him. The thought of him and I together made me happy. It calmed me and gave me a sense of security. I started driving myself crazy with all the 'what if's.' What if he loved me? What if he would make me happy? What if he was all I was looking for?

Gay kids fall for straight kids all the time, and it's not intentional, it just happens. You think someone is cute and you're lonely, so the thought of that comforts you. You wake up every day expecting someone to be on the other side of the bed. You check your phone expecting a "good morning baby :))" text, and it's never there. You forget who you are and you start to day dream about plans to go on a date on a Friday night, and then you have to snap back to reality and realize that you don't have a boyfriend. You have to face the fact that gay kids don't have a normal love life, and it's hard.

It's hard because sexuality isn't a visible thing. Yes, some people you can look at and notice their sexuality is very obvious, but not everyone falls into that stereotype. There are plenty of gay's and lesbian's who could pass for straight if they wanted to. It just makes an already confusing situation even more confusing. You find yourself wondering if any guy who gives you the slightest bit of attention likes you. You can't tell the difference between flirting and casual talk, because deep down, a part of you wants to believe that the guy talking to you is romantically attracted, but you know he isn't.

My problem with Luca was that he was one of those guys. I wanted him to like me so bad, because he was everything I wanted. It was driving me crazy, I started to overthink it all and I couldn't even handle it anymore. I couldn't get him off my mind because the thought of being with him soothed me. I was always so lonely and lacking affection. I mean the thought of being with Luca, the way my imagination raced as I pictured us together, it made me smile.

There's this old myth my grandparents believed in that said if you have someone on your mind, it means they're thinking of you, and that you should reach out to that person. I always dismissed it as a fake myth, like all the others. After all, my grandparents were very superstitious people. If you dropped a knife, you had to step on it or else you'd get into a fight, spilling salt meant bad luck, putting your shirt on inside out meant you were in for a surprise. None of it ever seemed legit, until that night.

At 2:45 a.m. my phone went off. At first, I

had the typical 'who the hell is this?' response, especially when I saw it was from an unknown number. It read:

"Hey, it's Luca from Spanish class. I was wondering if you wanted to hang out sometime?"

I was in shock. I didn't know what to say. I mean of course I wanted to hang out with him. I just didn't know how to talk to him without coming off as super cringy and overly interested. Sometimes that scares people off, and that's the last thing I wanted to do. I responded:

"Hey! Yeah of course!"

Once I hit send, my heart started pounding and I anxiously sat there waiting for a response, but I didn't wait long. He sent back:

"Can I come pick you up now?"

Now? I didn't know what to do, I mean I wasn't exactly the sneaking out type of kid. I was the kid who came home from school everyday and did my homework first thing before even getting a snack. I was the responsible mature kid who carried all the worries of a full grown adult because my parents always held me to such high standards. They always told me how I'd be the first one in the family to go to college and be successful. They always pushed me to be perfect, and I felt like my whole life was one big competition. I felt guilty to be a kid because it felt like I was letting my parents down. I had to be the responsible adult they wanted me to be, so I stood there for a couple seconds looking at the keyboard, deciding what to say. Without thinking, I began to type and I hit send:

"Yeah, can you come pick me up?"

What did I just do? He responded:

"Yeah, send me your address and wait out front."

I was really doing this, and as nervous as I was, it felt amazing. The adrenaline of doing something bad felt great. I threw on a pair of black joggers, and my favorite black hoodie, and than carefully made my way downstairs and out the front door. I sat down on the front steps waiting for a car to come up. It was so serene, I didn't even recognize it was my neighborhood. The busy streets were now empty with no cars. It was a chilly September night with a cool breeze. The only sounds were that of leaves in the wind and some crickets in the distance. The streets were lit up by lamp posts, but every single house was dark. I got so into everything around me, that when the car pulled up, I nearly had a heart attack because I forgot he was coming.

He stopped at the end of my driveway, because if he pulled in, his headlights would have shone right into my parents' windows and surely woken them up. So, I hustled across the lawn around the back of the car and to the passenger side where I gently closed the door shut.

It was awkward at first and I didn't know what to say. I'm assuming he didn't either because we drove for about five minutes in total silence before he pulled down this dead end and parked his car. He went into the trunk and pulled out this big beach blanket; it was navy blue with light blue stripes up and down the sides. He told me to follow him, and I did. We walked through some trees, using our phones as a makeshift light, and then we came out to a big opening. It was a field the size of two football fields with big tall grass that swayed in the cool breeze and made a faint rustling sound. There was the twinkle of fireflies that would occasionally spark up then vanish before reappearing in a new area. He laid down the blanket and we took off our shoes. We put one on each corner so it wouldn't lift up or blow away. We still hadn't talked much, but it was as if I could read his mind. We both got on the blanket and laid there holding hands.

The sky was exceptionally clear that night; like a black canvas with little spots everywhere. Except, those little spots were far away galaxies that had their own solar systems, and it really put into reality how small we really are. There are entire dimensions with endless possibilities of what could be inside them. What if there was another planet like Earth out there? What if on that planet everyone was happy, and there was no war, or hate, or crime? I know this all sounded like nonsense, but it got me thinking.

I got so into my thoughts that I just instinctively cuddled up next to Luca. I didn't even realize what I was doing. I guess it was because I felt comfortable around him, or something, I don't know. Without thinking, I rolled over, wrapped my arm around his body, and put my head on his chest. I had my ear right over his heart. I could hear it beating, and with every breath, he raised my arm with his stomach. He didn't do anything at first, he just let it happen, and then he finally spoke.

"You know, I'm really happy you came out with me tonight," he said.

"Me too," I said back.

"I wasn't sure if you liked me," he responded.

"I'm still in the closet so I don't like to make it obvious," I replied.

"Understandable."

After that, we went back to the silence, but it wasn't awkward. It was as if we were talking through signs. While holding hands, he started to gently rub his fingers over my knuckles. I responded by wrapping my leg over his and cuddling up even closer to him. We layed like that for a few before he turned his head and kissed me. It wasn't an expected kiss, it was a surprise, but sometimes surprises are the best. I know that one was. That was one of the moments in my life that I'd never forget.

I had never felt that close to another person before. I didn't have many friends growing up because I was a closeted gay guy. I liked what society would deem as 'feminine' things. I liked cooking, baking, and arts and crafts. I wasn't the race car fanatic or the try hard soccer player, and that made life hard. I could never talk to the straight guys because I always had to fake it, pretending to be something I wasn't. They'd all be talking about which teams made new trade-offs and who was gonna win the big champion games. Whenever a girl walked by, they'd all make a comment and I could just never see life from their perspective.

I preferred to have girl friends over guy friends, because I had more in common with girls than guys. The only problem was that they all thought I was straight, so they'd always take my platonic advances as romantic ones. I can't tell you how many times I'd have to deal with all the mixed messages. When I asked a girl to go to the mall with me, she thought it was a date, but I just wanted someone to shop with. So, if I wasn't rejected straight from the jump, I'd have to deal with the awkwardness of knowing that this girl thinks we're on a date.

I also didn't have that great of a family life. My mom was a short tempered know it all who had no patience and always yelled about everything. My dad, well, he was interesting. He was a negative person and he hated everyone. He never had a valid reason as to why he hated someone, it was always something stupid like "I could tell by the looks of 'em," and because of this, we never got along. We could never see eye to eye because I was a seventeen year old who wanted to get the most out of my life and he wanted to sit back on the sidelines and worry about other people and what they were doing with their lives while his just flew by.

It was always a fight wherever he went. He always had something to complain about, and to be honest, it was just plain out frustrating. It was annoying to have to fight so hard to think positive in an already negative world without someone constantly nagging in your ear. Everywhere we went, it was an issue. All black people were ghetto. I can't tell you how many times we'd walk into a store and see a black person and he'd comment about how they were taking over the neighborhood like it was some foreign invasion.

I can't tell you how many arguments we'd get into over his hate towards other people. For hours we'd sit there screaming at each other and never once did I break through to him, so I just gave up. It was so aggravating trying to make him understand. He always put a blame on someone else, but I just wanted him to realize it couldn't possibly be everyone else's fault. He was a bitter person and for the rest of his life he'll continue to stay that way unless something drastically changes, which I truthfully don't foresee happening.

It felt so amazing to be around someone who actually cared about me. Someone who saw me for something more than I was, and that's what true love is. True love is when someone sees you for more than just a person. They have the ability to see not only your body, but your mind, your heart, and your soul. They appreciate you as a person, and they acknowledge your independence and your capability to think on your own and have your opinions, and they respect that. They understand you and encourage you to go after and chase your dreams because they want what's best for you. Someone who'd choose your happiness over their own, who'd go out of their way to put a smile on your face and make life just a little bit less scary. I don't know how to explain it, but I felt all those things when I was with him, and when we were torn apart, it felt like my heart was being ripped out of my chest. I always thought of heartbreak as an emotional feeling, but it caused me literal pain as I sat there watching him get smaller and smaller in the distance as my parents drove me to that god-forsaken place.

I was talking to Luca for about two months when things got really serious and life felt amazing.

For the first time in a long time it felt like life was going the way it was supposed to. No negative thoughts or depressing behaviors. I didn't have to struggle to get out of bed in the morning. I wanted to do better for myself, and it was all because of him. He reassured me that I was good enough, which I shouldn't have needed another person's validation for, but that's how I was. I'd always been put down and viewed upon negatively. Luca was the only person in my life who actually made me feel like I mattered. Maybe that's because he was the only one who ever stuck around, or maybe it was the fact that he genuinely wanted what was best for me. We would sit there for hours talking about my dreams and goals. He'd encourage me, "Jake, I really think you can change the world. I think you'll be the one to break the cycle."

I loved spending time with him because it gave me a purpose again. Before him, my life was meaningless, but now I had a reason to live. The only frustrating part about the whole thing was it had to be done in secret. We couldn't walk in the park holding hands or go on cute dates. That's the reality of being gay in this world; you can't do what straight couples do. You can't kiss your boyfriend in public and not worry about becoming the next victim of a hate crime.

I think that's what annoys me the most because being a teenager is already stressful. You start driving and working, and you've got all these responsibilities now. You have to make sure you budget your money so that you can afford gas and all your other bills. You have to maintain your grades and apply yourself, not only academically, but in extracurricular activities so that you're well rounded for college. You have to sit down and literally choose what you want to do with the rest of your life and then figure out where and how you're going to get the education to make that happen.

Now, throw in being gay. All those previously mentioned things but add bullying, cyber-bullying, hate crimes, abusive families, and internal struggles from within yourself. You've got to grow up in a world that is the farthest thing from accommodating to you. Nobody understands you and they'll constantly downplay your problems and ignore your cries for help. Even if they wanted to help, they wouldn't be able to because they wouldn't get it. No straight person will ever know what it's like to be gay. There is absolutely no support for gay teens at all and people wonder why the substance abuse rate is higher in gay teens. It's because we can't talk about our problems and we have no outlet or safe space to vent. Most gay kids can't go to our parents and talk about our problems, and majority of us don't feel safe enough to talk about it in school because the fear of it getting out is greater than the need to actually speak your mind. The only real option we have is support groups. They are a guaranteed safe place where we can go and get actual support from people who've been in our shoes. We want someone who isn't going to sympathize with us, but someone who's going to treat us with the maturity to actually help us work through our problems. When you tell people what's going on and how you feel they tell you that they're sorry and it'll get better, but it doesn't. The thing is, we need help learning to cope and live with these things. We need help to learn how to rise above the hate rather than succumb to it and let it take over our lives.

Someone like me who needed support on dealing with unsupportive parents, but was left to figure it out on my own. I mean how are people like me supposed to live life like that? We are forced to hide who we really are, and we get up everyday pretending to be something we aren't. We have to learn to become a whole new person and wear this 'mask' that we can only take off when we're alone. It's like you're drowning in anxiety, depression, and negativity. You spend so much time thinking about the day your parents find out your gay and you think you have it all figured out on how it's gonna go, but when the time comes, it's nothing like you expected.

For me, it was an accident. I had no intention of telling them anything at first. Eventually, I realized how unrealistic that was and I decided that I'd do it when I graduated. I figured I'd go to another state for college, tell them and get that over with, and I wouldn't be there to deal with the repercussions. I didn't know what would go down, but I knew there'd be a lot of screaming and anger. I guess I underestimated how angry they'd really get because never in a hundred years did I think I'd be here.

My parents took me here the second they found out I was gay. It was Valentine's Day and my parents went out for dinner. I had the place to myself because Candace had broken up with me. I wasn't phased by it, to be honest. She claimed I was cheating on her because I was constantly sneaking around and never spent time with her. In reality, I was with Luca, so I guess technically that was cheating, but I don't know because I also never really viewed her as my girlfriend. I don't know what to think of the whole situation. It was very confusing and either way, it was bound to happen. I was just glad it was sooner than later.

Anyways, because I was alone, I had told Luca to come over. We were laying in my bed and I had my head resting on his shoulder. It was dark outside and we were watching a movie. Every time the scene changed, the room would go pitch black for a split second. It was one of those moments where I wasn't really paying attention to what was going on in the movie because I was taken back by the fact that I had finally done it. I finally found the person. I don't think either of us was actually paying attention to the movie, because before I knew it Luca and I were making out. It was intense, you think about that moment a lot and you think you're prepared for it, but when it happens it's overwhelming. So overwhelming that I managed to completely ignore the fact that my parents had come home.

It was all a blur, but I remember hearing the doorknob in my room jiggle, and thinking 'oh no!" but it was too late. I tried to jump up and get him out of the room but it wasn't possible. It was too late. Before I could even process what was going on, my father was standing in the doorway looking in total shock and disbelief. There was a moment of silence during which that shock and disbelief transitioned into anger and he just walked away. I didn't know whether to go after him or if I was better off staying there and waiting for him to come and talk to me. Luca could tell I was scared and he tried to comfort me, but nothing he could have done would have changed what just happened. I had just inadvertently come out to my parents.

I wanted to tell Luca to leave but I was debating on whether I actually wanted him to leave or not because he was probably the only person in the world I actually wanted to be around at that time. He was the only one in my life who understood me and could actually make me feel better. Before I could decide whether to let him stay, which he wanted to, or send him off, my father came running back into the room. This time I could hear his footsteps; his loud crashing footsteps. The footsteps of an angry enraged man storming into my room with a steak knife as he tried to kill my boyfriend. I couldn't even react. I just froze. What was I supposed to do?

There was so much yelling and emotions that I didn't even think and just jumped in between my father and Luca. I was two inches away from the tip of the blade as I was pressed as far up against Luca as I could, who was standing with his back against the wall. I was trying to calm my dad down, and my mother had now come in and was standing at the doorway crying hysterically. I could see her face between my dad's arms, which were ready to kill me. The only thing keeping him from shoving that knife straight into my skin was my right hand which was pushing back his hand.

I could feel my arm start to shake and get weak as I poured the last of my strength into one final push, which was able to knock my father back just enough to where he'd lose his grip and drop the knife. I just instinctively shoved Luca away and out the door. As I watched the love of my life run away, I felt sharp pain hit me in the head, followed by the sound of glass breaking. My eyesight went black for a second as I fell to my knees. I was able to open up my eyes for a split second as I touched my head, which was radiating a sharp pain. My head was wet, it was dripping, I could feel it running down my face. I looked down to see blood everywhere and then I blacked out.

When I woke up, I was at that horrible place. To be honest, my life had no purpose for the longest time. It was so dull and bleak that I couldn't help but feel that way myself, and then Jack showed up. Jack wasn't exactly smiling and gleaming with sunshine and joy but something about him gave me hope. I can't understand why, but his presence made me happy. Every time he walked into a room, it didn't matter what was going on, or whether I was having the worst day ever, he always managed to make it better.

There I was again, falling in love with another person who I had no business having feelings for. I tried to contain it, but it's hard to be friends with someone you love. It's a different type of pain when you fall in love with someone and you have to spend every day with them, knowing they'll never be what you want them to be.

He didn't know this, but I used to sneak out and hide behind the barn door while he talked to the animals. I never revealed myself because most of the stuff he talked about was personal, but it was empowering and inspirational. All this talk about changing the world and a better life. So, one day, I decided I'd tell him exactly how I felt.

"I just don't understand what's so hard about it? Why can't people just accept us? I mean, why is being gay a bad thing? How is me kissing a guy bothering anyone? I didn't ask for it. I didn't ask for any of this. Do they think I asked to be different? That I asked to be seen as the family screw up? That I wanted to be bullied and feel like trash all the time? I'm sick of it! I wish I could just fix it all!" Jack ranted.

"You can," I chimed in.

"Oh. Uh, how long were you there?" he turned around and asked embarrassingly.

"Not long," I said.

"Sorry," Jack said.

"It's nothing I haven't thought of myself," I responded.

"Why is this happening to us?" he questioned.

"I don't know," I answered.

There was an awkward silence where neither of us knew what to say. Then finally, he spoke.

"I'm just finishing up, then I'll meet you at the house," Jack said.

I gave in to an intense moment of emotions where I lost touch with reality. I forgot who I was and what that meant. A gay teen doesn't find love at the mall like straight couples. Very rarely does the guy you think is cute flirt back with you and it all works out perfectly. I didn't take into consideration that if I leaned in and kissed him, it might cause our world to go crashing down around us. So, I did it. I leaned in and kissed him expecting it to be this magical moment, but I felt regret and shame. I felt regret for doing it because I was brainwashed to think it was wrong, and the shame was because I couldn't believe I was doing something so disgusting.

I think that's when I really snapped and realized enough was enough! I shouldn't feel ashamed to kiss the person who makes me happy. I shouldn't feel wrong or disgusted for wanting to do what's right. I was tired of society brainwashing me to think that I was this monster, when I wasn't. Just because I wasn't your typical boy, it didn't invalidate me. I couldn't help that I found men attractive or that I found feminine styles more appealing than the regular graphic t-shirt and jeans. I was done with dealing with the stereotypical societal norms. That was it. I finally had enough and put my foot down.

Chapter 24
POV Jack

Jake kissing me changed everything. I mean it was great, don't get me wrong, but it also complicated things. As much as I wanted a relationship, it couldn't have worked, and I think we both knew that. However, we were two attention starved gay boys who found everything they were looking for in each other. He was cute and he made me smile. He was the only person to ever have faith in me, but it just couldn't have worked.

A relationship requires a lot. You can't be in one until you fix all your issues because insecurities lead to jealousy. Anger issues cause you to snap and lash out over the stupidest of things. Your mind isn't entirely there so you miss out on all the important moments and waste the time that you should be enjoying yourselves arguing. If you aren't emotionally stable it can ruin things, and let's be honest, neither of us were where we needed to be mentally. We had to work on ourselves before we could work on each other. Despite knowing all that, we both gave in and decided to give it a shot because love is the most powerful thing in this world. I knew how much pain and problems it would bring, but the way I felt with him in my arms almost made all of that feel worth it.

I think the biggest thing for me was that Jake's love filled my void of self hatred, and that was the most important thing to me. I would have done anything to not feel like a worthless piece of discard-able trash. I had no self respect, and I was at a point where I genuinely hated my-self. My weight wasn't good enough, my hair was too frizzy, I didn't have the perfect curls, and my features weren't perfect in just the right ways. I just wanted to feel important and validated, and I couldn't give myself that so I depended on Jake for it. He made me feel whole again. He assured me when I doubted myself. Whenever I felt down, he was there to pick me up. I became so dependent on him that the day he was ripped out of my arms

I vowed to never love again, and I stuck to that for a long time.

I'll never forget that day. It still hurts me to think about it. Jake and I used to write letters to each other to make it more subtle because this wasn't a place meant for bonding. I think if anything, our closeness would have brought a lot of unwanted attention and suspicions. So, we occasionally talked to try and convince everyone we were just casual buddy's, when in reality, we were far more than that. The letters were where we kept the more intimate stuff. To this day, when I'm feeling down, I go into my room and reach under my mattress to read them.

"I love you, stupid."

"There's times during the day where I just catch a glimpse of you from the corner of my eyes and I think 'damn, I'm lucky to have someone like him'."

"You're my everything."

"I'll love you forever and always, even if we argue or don't talk anymore. If it weren't for you, I don't know where I'd be."

They always made me smile. Then came the

guilt because I have to live with the fact that it was my smile that screwed up the whole thing. I didn't mean for it to go down like that, it's just he always managed to say something sweet or funny and I couldn't help it, and nobody ever noticed it, but that day they did. This big guy, I think his name was Marcus, I'm not sure. I tried to forget everything I could from that place, but he was the one who noticed it. From across the room, he came walking towards me.

Jake gave me that look and I knew I had to do something, so I tried to fold it up and stick it in my shoe but it was useless. Anywhere else if they saw someone reading a piece of paper and laughing they would have just walked away moving on with the rest of their day, but not there. He came right up to me and gave me a look as if to tell me he knew something was up. I just sat there looking at the ground. I didn't even try to acknowledge him.

He then put his hand out, I knew what he wanted, but I wasn't about to give it to him. I prayed in my head that maybe he'd walk away if I just played stupid, so I gave him a very confused look, as if to say 'what are you doing?' but he wasn't having it. He took it upon himself to grab my leg, right behind the knee. I tried kicking, but the way he had me was useless. He ripped my shoe right off, my laces tied and all, even taking my sock off with the force he used to just yank it off. Once it was off, he shook it and out fell the paper. The crumpled up little piece of paper. He didn't say a word, he just walked away and up the stairs.

The whole time he was gone, Jake and I didn't say a word. We knew what was about to happen.

"Don't panic, we knew this might happen," Jake said.

He was surprisingly calm, given the extremity of what was going on. I don't know if maybe he came to terms with it, or maybe he had been preparing for something like that, I'm not sure. I, on the other hand, was totally blindsided. I had no idea what to say or do. I wanted to say so much but the lump in my throat made it so I could just about breathe. Jake was just sitting there when he did what he does best, he gave me the look. The look that told me everything was going to be alright. That he understood what I was thinking in my head, even though I couldn't come out and say it.

He did his half smirk and pulled me in close so I could lean my head on his shoulder. As he wrapped his arm around me, he said, "we had a good run didn't we?" The intensity of that feeling of connection I felt in those moments is something I'll never forget. Something that, to this day, still gives me goosebumps. I began to say my goodbyes to him in my head. I told him how much I loved him and needed him. How empty my life would be without him there at my side. There was a lot more I wanted to say, but all my thoughts began to scramble together to the point that nothing made sense.

I'd like to say that I made peace with it, but I didn't. I still wake up in the middle of the night, shaking, drenched in a cold sweat from nightmares I have of that night. Not having any closure was the worst part of it. There was so much more I really wanted to do and see with him, like live a real life in the real world. I can only imagine what that would be like now, and it hurts. It hurts to not know what could have been the rest of my future with him.

I'll never forget the sound of those chains rattling as the deadbolt on the door clicked open and my heart dropped. I knew right then and there that this was it. When the door opened, I heard a couple voices all talking in a low grumble, followed by the footsteps of four men as they walked down those old creaky stairs. That was it, that was good-bye forever.

It was all downhill from there. Naturally, my flight or fight instincts kicked in as four lumber jack sized men cornered me up against a wall. Realistically, there was no use in even trying. However, I wasn't ready to give up. I couldn't just give up. There was a tiny space in between two of them, that if I could manage to slip through, I'd have a clear shot up the stairs and to the open unlocked door. It was a very pathetic attempt that failed miserably, because before I could even take one step, I felt a pair of hands wrap around me and my whole body flung forward as I was tackled from behind.

I have no recollection of anything after that. I just remember waking up in my own bed back at my house to my mom and dad standing over me. As I slowly began to open my eyes, it became more conscious of where I was. At first, it hurt my eyes because they hadn't adjusted to the brightness of my room with the window wide open as sunshine beamed in. I began to make more and more sense of the situation until it finally clicked. I was home!

I didn't have much energy in me, and I still felt sort of weak, but I managed to sit up. To my surprise, both my parents were there waiting for me, and they seemed sort of happy I was back.

"Sweetie, relax. Here, take a sip of this," she said as she handed me a glass of lukewarm water from my nightstand.

As I sipped on it, I could see my dad's skeptical facial expressions. "Is it really you son?"

"Yeah, it's me," I said slightly smiling.

"I can't believe it, he's really fixed!" my dad exclaimed.

Have you ever hit rock bottom and thought to yourself, 'it can't get any worse than this,' and every time without fail, it always manages to somehow get worse? My father just took my pain and amped it up to a thousand. The fact that he cared more about my sexuality and being 'saved' than the fact I was being eaten alive by guilt, pain, rage, and suffering killed me. You can only block out all the insults, backhanded compliments, and negativity for so long that you eventually get to a point where it just keeps adding on and on and it starts to break you. Each insult breaks your charisma and your self respect. Your heart and mind are shattered and it feels like someone is stepping on the pieces.

What hurt the most was that most of my pain was coming from my parents, the very people who put me in this world. Friends, and even sometimes family, come and go, but your parents are supposed to be the ones who never leave your side. Yet, here mine were, watching me eternally die and all they could care about was whether or not I was 'normal.'

I had a choice to be brave and tell them no, and that no matter what they said or did, I'd always be this way. Or, I could have taken the path of lying. So, I chose to lie, and I did it because I physically didn't have the courage or the strength to be brave. Lying didn't weaken me or invalidate me. I was still gay, that would never change. It's just I couldn't bear the fact of knowing that if I told them I'd have to live knowing that I was viewed as some pathetic mistake of a reject. I believe that one day I'll come out, I just don't know when.

People often mistake that as cowardly to lie, but let me tell you, it is most definitely not. Lying comes with its own set of problems. I had to learn to bite my tongue a lot, learn to suppress the things that made me, me. I woke up everyday hating who I was, knowing exactly who I wanted to be, but unable to make any of the changes to fix my life. It was an endless loop of knowing exactly what the problem was, and exactly how to fix it, but being totally clueless on how you'll find the courage to do it. You hope that one day you will wake up and it'll be there, but everyday it's the same. I didn't know how to cope with it, I was overwhelmed with all these emotions, and then one day, I discovered drugs.

I had ordered a hoodie offline, and when it came, I opened the package and went upstairs to try it on. It fit well, it wasn't anything crazy, it was just a basic pink hoodie. I was standing there in the mirror, fixing it so that all the wrinkles weren't bunched up, when my father passed by and noticed.

"You're joking right?" my father said.

I didn't know what to say. I was confused and taken back, so I just gave him a look as if to say "what are you talking about?"

"Take that off right now!" he yelled.

"What? Why?" I said defensively.

"Take that thing off!" he yelled again.

"I don't understand what's wrong?" I questioned.

"I said take it off!!" he shouted.

"Okay!" I shouted back.

I didn't know why he was freaking out, but I figured I'd just take it off so I didn't have to hear his mouth.

"No son of mine is gonna walk around wearing a pink shirt! What are you a fag?" my father said, ripping the shirt out of my hand and storming off.

I tried to keep my cool, and I thought I had it under control, but only for a split second before I lost it.

"Is that what this is about? A pink shirt?" I followed him out of the bathroom.

"It's not just a pink shirt, it's the fact you think it's okay to walk around disgracing this family and embarrassing us! Do you not see what this is doing to us? You and your stupid 'gay' decisions. Can't you see it's tearing us apart? I don't know why you can't just be normal!" my father said.

I knew he wasn't the type of guy to pick a fight with, but I just couldn't help my anger. What kind of a world do we live in where the color of a shirt makes you gay? What is wrong with our society that we have to genderize things like clothing? That a guy can't just wear pink clothing without being assumed as gay? It just bothered me so bad because I was tired of hiding myself, so to avoid an argument or saying something that I knew would get me in trouble, I walked away. I put on my slides and walked out the front door. I didn't know where I was going, but I knew I couldn't be in my house a moment longer or I would have exploded.

I walked for about twenty minutes before I came up to this construction site for a new shopping center. The front of the store was facing one of the highways and had easy access to the big parking lot from the main road so that they could do business when it opened, but the back was completely wooded. There was a big empty black garbage pod that was filled with pieces of discarded wood. My first thought was 'let's break things.' I was just so angry and I had so much built up in me that I couldn't help it. So, I walked over to the wall of the pod that was about a half of a foot over my head and looked up at the pieces that extended from the top. I reached on my tip toes to grab the edge that was cut rather clean. I'm assuming it was the scraps from the saw. Once I had it in my hand, I started walking backwards pulling it out with me. Then finally, it clanked on the ground. It was a big six foot piece of plywood. I grabbed it by one end and held it in the air. I felt like I had so much power, but it was only a piece of wood.

I walked over to the big solid brick wall and started swinging. "CRACK, CRACK, CRACK." I just kept swinging, and with each hit, it splintered into a smaller piece until I had a little nub left in my hand. At first, I hit it lightly and I almost had to put effort into it, but with each hit after that, I got more and more power. I was swinging and screaming and just so annoyed at life. I got so angry that everything just went black, but I still kept swinging, and when I ran out of wood, I turned to my fists. I banged them up against the wall, not feeling anything, until I eventually was able to see clearly enough to look down at my bloody split open knuckles. It didn't hurt, it just mildly stung, but I could tell it was going to bruise because it had already started to turn blue and yellow.

After that, I just collapsed to the ground. I was done. I had given up. It was all too much. I was frustrated and disgusted. I was tired of being led on by false hopes. These politicians and civil rights movement leaders would talk about upcoming changes, but everyday went by and I never really saw my life change. I was still the victim of a broken and flawed system. If they really wanted to fight for equality, why hadn't they already made the inhumane practices of conversion therapy illegal? Why hadn't they outlawed the Panic Defense Law? Why wasn't LGBTQ+ history being taught about in schools all across the country? It was all an excuse to pass off as a halfway decent person when, by not doing anything, they were in fact becoming the very problem by enabling the hate and the violence and condoning it. Someone who is truly against inequality would do everything in their power to make sure such things didn't happen. Yet, here are those people who claim to be all for equality, who are some of the most powerful people in the world, and they sit back knowingly aware of what's going on but they don't do a thing.

They say to speak up about the social injustices and I did. I created petitions, wrote letters and emails, but all of it was just swept away. I wrote to several major News organizations and politicians. I even made posts addressing some of the more pressing issues hoping someone would see it and agree with me, but every time, it just got swept away. My videos and posts talking about how the alarmingly high rate of suicide in gay teens was rising had only gotten fifteen likes. Meanwhile, all it took was some hot dude with six packs to flex his muscles on an app and he somehow got three million likes. I began to drive myself crazy wondering why no one else saw things the way I did. Was it because I wasn't hot enough? Was it as simple as that nobody cared? How could anyone be okay with what was going on?

I'd challenge you to read the suicide note of a sixteen year old who killed themselves solely because of their sexuality and still hold those view points that we don't need change. Sit down and talk to the kids who are mentally, verbally, and physically abused, and tell them you don't see a need for immediate change. Talk with the boy who came out to his dad and almost got killed if it wasn't for his mother prying the knife out of her husbands hand as he had it pressed up to his gay sons neck. Attend the wedding of a young girl who has no father to walk her down the aisle, not because he passed away, but because he refused to support her and her wife. I want you to imagine all of the broken hearted fragile kids out there right now who have no hope in the future unless a change is made.

My heart hurts because I want nothing more than to make that change for them, because I know the pain, and it's the worst. I tried and tried, but every time, I fell short. I didn't have the capabilities to change the world, so I gave up when I should have kept fighting. I crawled up into a ball on the ground of that empty construction site and gave up. I was done. What was the point? People were just going to keep suffering and dying, and everyone would look and say "what a shame," but nobody would actually ever be brave enough to stand up and make the changes we needed. I felt like I was the only one who actually could, but there was this impossible force blocking me from doing it. Why would I even try and fight something that big? I had no odds in my favor, so I let go. I let go and drifted away. When I came to, there were these two girls standing over me and I nearly jumped out of my skin. The girl on the right, Girl 1, was insanely skinny to the point where her collar bone stuck out and I could have probably fit my hands around her waist from thumb to thumb. She had her hair split dyed, the right side was a jet black, and the left a platinum blonde. She was wearing a pair of rainbow slip-on shoes, with black leggings, a grey whitewashed graphic tee, and a rose gold zip up hoodie. The hoodie was open and she had it half on and half off so that it almost draped off her shoulders.

The girl on the left, Girl 2, was a bit heavier. She had a fuller face, chubby cheeks, and frizzy knotted dark brown hair. She wore glasses that seemed to cover her rather small eyes, and she had freckles all over her face. She was wearing baggy sweatpants and an over sized tie dye t-shirt. They seemed harmless, but no matter how you look at it, you're going to be scared when you wake up to two strangers looking at you.

"Hey, relax. We aren't gonna bother you," Girl 1 said.

"Who are you guys?" I said as I sat up and rubbed my eyes so that I could make sense of what was going on.

"Who are you?" Girl 2 asked.

"Jack," I responded.

"Well what are you doing in our spot?" Girl 2 said.

"Your spot?" I questioned.

I hadn't noticed, but on the one girl's shoulder was a backpack they put on the ground and opened. It was filled with a bunch of random things. At first, I was really confused until she reached into the front pouch and pulled out a little plastic baggie with two grams of marijuana in it. Then it clicked, and I realized I was in a very awkward situation.

"Ohhh, I'm so sorry. I-I-I-I can go," I stuttered.

"No stay." Girl 1 said smiling.

"I couldn't, I don't have any money on me." I said.

By now, I could tell based on her facial expressions that the girl on the left wanted me gone, but her friend ignored her and continued on trying to get me to stay.

"Have you ever smoked before?" Girl 1 asked.

"No," I responded.

"Then maybe-," Girl 2 began.

"Don't be silly. The first time's on me! There's no time like the first time so enjoy it," Girl 1 cut her off.

With that said, they reached into their bag of junk and started pulling out all of what appeared to be junk. A big extra large 32 oz. soda cup from a gas station, a lighter, an empty scrunched up crinkled water bottle, a pocket knife, and another water bottle that she said had a mixture of grapefruit juice and water. When I asked why, she said it gave it a flavor and didn't make it taste as strong. I wasn't sure if that was true, but I wasn't about to criticize and ask questions, so I just sat back and watched the process.

She started off by pouring the water mix into the big soda cup, filling it to about three quarters of the way full. She then put the empty bottle to her mouth and blew into it, restoring it back to its original shape. After cutting some holes into the bottom of it, she placed the bottom into the big soda cup and placed the weed onto the cap of the bottle. She held the lighter up to it, and as it burned, the smoke went into the inside of the bottle until the clear plastic became cloudy. That was my first ever time smoking.

She told me to hurry up and put my lips around the top of the bottle before the smoke went away, so I did. She told me to inhale, but to hold it for as long as I could. Following her orders, I took a deep breath and the smoke disappeared from the inside of the bottle into my lungs, almost like it vanished without a trace. Once it was inside of me, I felt this weird tickling feeling, almost like a cough, but instead of it coming from my throat, it was coming from deep inside of my chest. I held it as long as I could counting each second go by, 'one, two, three, four, five, six, seven, eight,' and just as I hit nine, I erupted in the worst coughing fit ever. Coughs that came from deep parts of my diaphragm, while my throat burnt and my stomach was sore. I began to think, 'what is all the fun in this?' When I looked over, both of them were smirking.

"Don't be discouraged, just try it again," Girl 1 said.

I was skeptical, but I figured maybe I had done it wrong, so I nodded my head in agreement. She took the lighter, just like before, filling the bottle with smoke, and just like before, I put my lips into it and took a deep inhale. 'One, two, three, four, five, six, seven, eight, nine, ten, eleven, twelve, thirteen, fourteen, fifteen.' Fifteen was my limit. Upon my exhale, I could see the smoke come out of my mouth and it went smoothly. I mean, I had a little bit of a tingle in the back of my throat, but it wasn't anything like the first time.

"See what I mean?" Girl 1 asked.

"Are you feeling it yet?" Girl 2 questioned.

"I don't think so. I don't know. I've never been high before," I responded.

"One more hit," Girl 1 said.

That last hit was the worst. As soon as the smoke hit the back of my throat, I felt light headed, like I was going to pass out. I didn't even make a full inhale before I turned over and started to dry heave. Then like magic, it hit me. I was high. For the first time in months I smiled. I remembered what it felt like to be me, a feeling I thought was gone forever. I mean I'd legit gone through periods where I forgot what smiling felt like and I literally couldn't laugh. I would be sitting there angry at the fact that I couldn't be happy or let go. I always had a worry on my mind and I couldn't just focus on what was going on in the present. I always had to worry about the future or sit there and sulk over the past.

I had tried so hard in the past to fix it. I followed all the stupid advice they give you, "think positive," "do the things the make you happy," "embrace the small things." I tried and tried but nothing worked, except drugs. They were the cure all that seemed to make it all go away. Realistically, drugs weren't the answer. Realistically, all drugs did was numb the effects of the pain, but once they wore off, the pain would still be there. That's how they get addicting because you enjoy the feeling of no pain, and for someone like me, being sober is nothing but pain.

If I was taught other coping mechanisms, I would have used them, but I wasn't. There weren't any gay support groups where I could talk to other people like me who were going through the same things I was. There wasn't anyone there to check in on my mental health and to make sure I was doing alright. With such a bad stigma around it, I was afraid to ask for help. We are so quick to throw labels on everything nowadays that it makes it harder to get help. I genuinely thought that only crazy people saw therapists or psychiatrists, but the truth is, there are many normal people who need the services that they offer.

You don't have to be crazy or mentally ill to talk about your mental health. When someone gets physically ill, do we label them as disabled? No, we don't because we understand that they still have some capabilities and that at the time being, a current part of them isn't working right. So rather than tear them down and make them feel worse, we help them get to a doctor and we help get them better. Mental health isn't like that. In society's eyes, you're either crazy or you're not. There is no in between.

You don't have to just be gay to have mental health issues. These types of things affect everyone: straight people, gay people, white people, Black people, Asian, Hispanic. It's not a pick and choose type of thing. It's just the fact that life in general is stressful, and when you add the issues that gay people, and people of color have to face, it makes it more common for them to have depression, anxiety, and stuff like that. How could anyone have a positive mindset when everyday they wake up and see the injustices being done to them and their community, and they know that nothing is being done about it?

All the stress, the negativity, the pain, combined with the lack of support and the lack of knowledge on how to cope with it causes kids like me to turn to other things. We try to create artificial happiness from drugs, alcohol, and sex. Things that, no matter what, will constantly feel good. It makes perfect sense. I was miserable until I got high, then all of a sudden I felt happiness. Why would I stop?

The real me that I had been suppressing for so long finally came out. I was my funny, witty, sarcastic self. My mind cleared of all the worrying about stupid, unimportant stuff that typically fogged my head. I was in the clear to be me. I found myself physically unable to stop smiling. Cheesing so hard to the point that it hurt, and the more I thought about it, the more I smiled. I was smiling because I was smiling, as confusing as that sounds, it all felt so great.

When I went home, I was afraid my family would notice, but then I realized that my parents really didn't care that much about me. I was just sort of there. I was always home alone so I smoked a lot, and when they were home I still smoked, just more discreetly. I lived in a mansion. There were rooms in my house that my parents hadn't been in for months. They didn't exactly make it hard.

My one time experience smoking in the back of a construction site quickly turned into a marijuana addiction, and from there, it spiraled down. It went from weed, to mixing it with alcohol. The occasional drink and a blunt was satisfying, but that didn't last long. I was at a point where I was smoking a blunt and a half a bottle a day. The more my parents went away, and the more freedoms I had, the worse it got. The weed turned to pills, and the pills into coke, and before I knew it, I was dabbling in a bit of everything. I was sharing needles with strangers, and just doing anything I could to get high.

The weed and the alcohol became light weight stuff, so I moved up. I was taking just about anything I could buy off the streets all for a cheap thrill. I was trying to replace the loneliness in my life with drugs. I was trying to make happiness in situations where I didn't have any. All it was, was a band-aid on a knife cut because everyday when I'd wake up sober, or halfway sober, and I'd start to feel those feelings, I'd realize that my intoxicated world didn't exist. No matter how many times I did it, each and every time felt the same.

For a very long time, I struggled with the battle of loneliness. Then one day, I met Alex, and he changed my life. I was scrolling online when I found a link to an anonymous male escort site. Curious, I decided to check it out. It was almost like shopping for a car. All these men with pictures and bios, the fetishes they had and what to expect if I were to 'purchase' them for the night. Money wasn't an issue. I could have bought all of them, but only one caught my eye, and that was Alex. It had nothing to do with his looks, and to be honest, I didn't even read his bio. It was more like this gut feeling that told me to pick him, so I did. I put in the credit card information, devised this whole plan so that nobody would know what I was doing, and that was it, I had done it.

The next two days I sat for hours nervously waiting, and when the time actually came, I was shaking from all the anxiety. I walked out back by the circuit breaker and waited, and waited, and waited. I'm not a patient person, so I began to panic. When I panic, my thoughts start to race and I get so discombobulated that I start to get enraged by all the confusion and it just never ends well for me. What if this was all a scam? Why did I do this? What was I trying to prove?

I knew I was gay, I'd been turned on by men before. I guess I just wanted to prove it. Saying I was gay when I had never had sex with a guy felt almost like a lie. I needed to have had sexual intimacy in order to be gay, which looking back on now, I know that isn't true. Sex doesn't validate your sexuality. The term gay doesn't only mean same sex, sex. It means same sex relationship as well. I loved guys before. Take Jake for example, I would have done anything for him. I'd been attracted when the hot actor takes off his shirt during a beach scene in a movie. I would get all flustered and blush when I saw a cute guy staring at me. All of this made me gay, but I didn't have anyone to tell me this, so I told myself that having sex with Alex was the only way to finally be gay.

When I finally saw him, I wouldn't say I was happy, but more relieved. I didn't need to talk to him or be around him long before I could tell he was broken. He had the darkest circles under his eyes and the saddest of looks on his face. Actually, I wouldn't describe it as 'sad,' but rather dead. He had no facial expressions, no emotion, just a lifeless face. On the other hand, I enjoyed that lifeless face. It grew on me and I started to enjoy his company. I enjoyed it because he was almost like a puppet. He sat there doing nothing. I had full control over him and I loved it.

I never had control over my life. I always had someone tell me what to be or how to act. With

Alex, I finally had that control. Not only did he give me control, but he gave me a sense of being needed. I told myself that if it weren't for me, who'd feed Alex and make sure he took a shower. His boyfriend clearly sucked, so I ended that for him and I took over.

I won't get too personal, but the sex was great. I had years of sexual oppression built up that I was finally able to release. I loved every second of my time with him. I'm OCD about a lot of things, one of them being I'm very structured. I love schedules and routines, which at times can make me controlling. I love to take charge because I see a perfect way for things to be done and perfection satisfies me. If it isn't perfect, I almost get what feels like an itch in my brain and I go nuts. My anger kicks in and I start yelling and doing all these crazy things I don't even realize.

Alex let me take charge. He didn't argue when I told him what to do. He didn't tell me I was bossy or too demanding, he just sat there. My parents were gone for six months to set up a new office out of the country. I had all the time in the world with Alex, and I don't think I ever felt more happy. Aside from Jake that is, but I tried my best to forget about him. Alex was the new Jake. Alex became my everything very quickly. I woke up to take care of Alex. I got dressed and showered so that I could look good for Alex. Everything was about Alex. I wouldn't say I had an obsession with him, more like I wanted it to work so bad.

If gay relationships were normal, and I had as many options as a straight guy to choose from, I wouldn't have been doing what I was doing. The thing is, when you're gay and you're one of the lucky ones to find a boyfriend, you don't let him go. You stay because you realize the physical pain of being alone is worse than the emotional pain of a toxic relationship. I couldn't just walk into a store and flirt with the closest guy I saw, like most people do. I had to fear that if I did that, and the guy was straight, he would punch me in the face. I had to deal with the constant battle of if they were just being kind to me or flirting, and I never really knew the real answer. Alex was a blessing to me, and I didn't want to let him go.-*

I felt guilty at first because I knew Alex wanted to leave me, but in a way, I felt like I was the best thing for him. It was mutual and we both helped each other out. I gave him drugs and food, and bought him things, and he kept me company. He made my life a little less lonely. He was the only one in the entire world that understood me, and if for a second I thought that any of this would have hurt him, I would have stepped up and done something. Then, the time came when I realized that I wasn't helping him, and he wasn't helping me. In fact, we were destroying each other and we didn't even know it.

As for me, Alex was unintentionally enabling all of my bad behaviors. I used to get mad at people when they contradicted me or told me I was wrong, but that's exactly what I needed. Someone like Alex would just let me be me and not tell me I needed help. They'd let me sit there and drive myself crazy until I eventually exploded and had a nervous breakdown. Alex, however, was the true victim. I had turned him into a a monster. He wasn't talking or doing anything for himself.

I'd sit there for hours having conversations and he'd be staring off into space high as a kite seeing hallucinations. I tried to tell myself that was normal. I said that if he was going to do this, which, based on the way he looked when I first met him, he was already planning on doing it, then at least he'd be doing it with me at his side. Someone who was experienced in those types of things, someone who wouldn't give him laced stuff off the streets and wouldn't let him rot away in an alley.

I never wanted that for him. I loved him. I hated to admit it, but I loved him. I loved him because that's what he needed. He needed someone to love him and take care of him while he checked out for a little bit. He needed that break to escape from reality, and that's when it hit me, he was me. I was Alex, and I knew what road he was heading down because I was currently walking that path. So, I made the hardest decision of my life and I decided enough was enough.

I didn't want to be like this anymore. I needed help. None of this was my fault. I didn't ask for any of it, but nonetheless, it was up to me to hold myself together and make sure I didn't let it get the best of me. I could see the path I was heading towards, the path Alex was on, and I knew if I didn't do it then, I would wind up being just another number or statistic. So, I reached out for help and checked myself into a facility.

I packed up the car, gave Alex some cash, and dropped him off outside of a shelter. He was still high when I left him, and part of me felt like I was obligated to finish what I started, but I couldn't help myself and I knew I'd only let him down. I gave him the biggest hug you could ever imagine, got in the car, and drove off. The whole time I watched him in the rear view mirror as he got smaller and smaller until he disappeared.

I guess that was goodbye, but it didn't feel like a goodbye. At least not the goodbye I had with Jake. No, this felt a little less traumatic and more positive because I knew he was going to get help. With Jake, it was uncertain what would happen next. With Alex, I knew was going to get better, and I knew, somehow, he'd find his way, get right, and be okay. He had to, he was a survivor, we all were. This was the beginning of a new life. I

I was determined to do better for myself so that I could speak up and change the world. We live in America, 'home of the free, land of the brave,' but what is so free about a country that implements the legal practice of conversion therapy? What is so brave about sitting back and letting people die? I had to get better to make the changes that we all needed. I was tired of empty promises, so I decided

I would take it into my own hands to stand up and rise above all the hate.

Chapter 25
POV Connor

After I got out of the hospital, I spiraled out of control. I mean bad, like I didn't know if I'd ever be okay again. It started off with just always thinking about him and thinking about how special he made me feel. Before I met him, I felt worthless, like I didn't matter, and he changed that. Having him there gave me a sense of confidence, a sense of meaning. He made me feel like I mattered, and when he left, he took that with him. I felt like I was trash because I just couldn't understand why he would leave me. Why did he choose a stranger over me? Was I really not good enough? That's always been my biggest fear in life; that I'd never be good enough. I've always feared that I'd never find love or happiness because I wasn't enough, and after overthinking for some time, I convinced myself that was true. I told myself that I was a horrible monster and nobody would ever love me or like me because of all the problems I had. I was awkward, I never knew how to make small talk, and I didn't understand social cues. To most people, socializing is like riding a bike; once you learn it's super easy and you never forget, but I never learned how to ride a bike.

While he was in my life, I felt great. I felt like I was on top of the world because I finally felt good enough. I finally found what I'd been looking for for so long; happiness. Just knowing that I mattered to someone gave me purpose. He made me feel like I had to keep trying because, to be honest, I'd given up on life a long time ago. With Alex in my life, I felt like I couldn't give up because he was counting on me. When he left, all that changed.

I started drinking, even after the accident, and the doctors told me not to. I went to the liquor store, bought a big handle of vodka, and everyday I'd start my day off with a shot. Well, I don't know if it was a shot or not because I never used an actual glass. I just took a quick swig from the bottle. It would burn as it went down, tasting like a flavored rubbing alcohol, and it would leave a weird tingling taste in my mouth.

Drinking was the first thing I did, but after that it got worse. I remember my head hurting from constantly thinking. All I could think was, 'you aren't enough. He chose someone else over you because you aren't enough.' I was so frustrated because I just wanted to scream, but I couldn't, because I felt too weak. I tried to, believe me, I tried. I locked myself in the bathroom, turned on the shower to the hot water and let the steam fog up the whole bathroom. I had a whole playlist of sad songs going and I kept trying to push myself to let it all out but I couldn't. I sat there for twenty minutes going over all the reasons my life sucked, trying to get myself mad enough to the point where I could just let it all out, but I couldn't do it.

I think I bottled it all up for so long that I couldn't let it out. I would get so upset that I could feel the tears building up, and just as I was about to bawl my eyes out, I'd tense and they'd go away. I needed to find some sort of way to release my feelings. I just couldn't figure out what to do and it was driving me crazy. The more I thought about it, the more alone I felt. The more alone I felt, the worse it got. I couldn't just shut off my brain. I wished I could but it wasn't that easy.

I did small things to distract myself every time I thought of him. It would only last for like ten minutes before the thought of him, and how happy I was, came popping back into my head. I just wished I could forget him, but I couldn't. He was all I ever thought about. The first thing I did every morning for a week after he left was check my phone to text him good morning. I'd open my messages, expecting to see our chats at the top of the list on my recent conversations, but with each day, it got lower and lower until I didn't even see his name. Every time my phone went off I'd check it right away to make sure it wasn't him. I knew he was gone, but I still had this sick twisted idea that maybe he'd come back. Some last bit of hope, but deep down, I knew it was over.

Just when I thought it couldn't get worse, it did. I was scrolling through my phone and a picture of him with my replacement came up. I almost vomited from the knot that formed in my stomach. I started shaking and I felt the tears build up. I thought maybe this time it would happen, maybe

I'd finally let it all out, but I was wrong. I just sat there as a single tear rolled down my face and hit my hand. All of our happy moments flashed before me: the late night calls, the checking up on me to make sure I was having a good day, all the 'I love you's,' and every hug and kiss. It was all just gone. I was gone, and the worst part was that he seemed happy. Was I that easy to forget? How could I have been over here with my heart hurting and he was just so nonchalant about it? It was right then and there that I knew my worst fears had come true; I wasn't enough. I was so easy to forget because of how irrelevant I was. Everyone always forgot about me and moved on so quickly because I was worthless. I didn't need to convince myself that I was useless. I now knew it to be true, and it sucked.

I was self harming, drinking, spiraling down a really dangerous road, and I didn't think I would come out on the other side of it. I wanted to give up so badly, but this tiny little part of me just told me to keep fighting, even though I had no reason to keep going on. I just had this tiny feeling that it was gonna get better. So that night, I packed up my things in one suitcase and left. I had no idea where I was going, I just needed to leave there. I got on a bus that I had no idea where it was going and I took off on my next journey.

The bus was rather full but there were two empty seats. One seat was next to this man who was coughing, sneezing, and had dirty tissues everywhere. All the way in the back there was the other empty seat next to this guy. He was super skinny and short with long straight black hair that covered his entire face. He was curled up in the seat with his knees to his chest and a blanket wrapped around him as he laid his head against the window. When I sat down, he gave me a sort of death glare. I was debating about taking my chances with the sick man, but the bus had already taken off so I just sat there with my legs pointed outwards toward the aisle to give him as much room as possible.

We went the whole two hour bus ride without speaking. He was watching videos on his phone and, I'm not going to lie, I was being nosy and watching as well. When his phone died, I didn't say anything. I just reached into the front part of my bag and pulled out my portable charger to hand it to him. He took it without saying anything and went back to watching videos. He was odd, but I could tell he wouldn't hurt a fly. He seemed a lot like me; misunderstood by the rest of the world. I got a feeling that him and I would get along really well, he just needed to let loose a little. He seemed uptight, almost like he was afraid of opening up, and believe me, I know that feeling. So, I decided that he'd be my first friend in my new life.

As the night went on and the bus went through it's stops, we came to the last one. It was only me and this mystery guy on the bus. He still hadn't said one word, so I just gave up. I mean I didn't even know his name, so I got up, grabbed my bag, and left. I walked all the way down the empty aisle and stepped outside to the fresh air, which was a relief from that musty bus. It was cold out and I had no idea where I was. Other than that, I was on the side of a highway and the only thing open was a diner.

I stood there for a second, trying to get myself together to figure out where I was. I turned on my phone to check my location. When I looked down to my lock-screen and I saw the picture of the two of us smiling from our trip to Florida all that while back I lost it. Every happy memory I ever had came back to me. Along with all of the nasty fights and ugly mornings. All the pain, the anger, the rage, I wouldn't have traded any of it. I just wanted to be with him. I wanted him there with me.

I missed all the nights where I'd be laying in bed, overthinking something stupid, and he'd come tiptoeing down the hallway all quiet, trying not to wake me up. He'd shimmy his way to the bed, in the dark, so as not to wake me up from the light, and he'd sit on the side of the bed. Every night he did this, like clockwork. He'd take his shoes off, never untying them, just pulling them right off with his socks, and then he'd get into bed. He'd lift up the blanket, just enough so that he could slide up next to me and press himself gently against my back. He'd wrap his cold hand across my side and over to my chest where he'd gently play with the ends of my hair. He would twirl the little curls around his finger until he fell asleep. I would lay there, pretending to sleep while he did all this, and I just felt safe. I would have done anything for that feeling again, and a small part of me believed I would. I truly believed that one day, I'd find him again and we'd pick up where we left off. For a second, I sat there taking that all in. Then the phone rang and it was all gone. That dream, that hope, was torn right out of my hands.

Chapter 26
POV Ian

*My name is Ian, but my old name was Chris*tine. Yup, I'm transgender. It's still a lot to get used to. There's times when people call my name and I don't even pay attention because I think they're talking to someone else. Or, sometimes when I'm in a store and a mother or father is talking to their daughter and they call out her name "Christine?" I'll turn around. It's like I still can't adapt to it yet, which is funny because I'll never forget the day I made it official. I hadn't come out yet but I was ready. I just needed to find a name. I was way overthinking it, I didn't want anything too basic. My first thought was 'well my name's Christine, I'll just become Chris,' but something about the name Chris didn't sound right to me. I was online for hours looking at lists of guy names for trans guys and none of them stood out to me. I was at a total loss staring at that computer screen for hours reading off names from a list. I started to get a headache so I decided to go for a walk.

I was walking around my neighborhood all the way to the end of the cul-de-sac a couple blocks down from my street. We lived by the shore, so two streets down from us all of the houses were waterfront on the lagoon, which if you went all the way down, opened up into the bay. I was walking on the right side of the road so that I could see oncoming traffic, and as I walked, I could see the sun setting and the sky turning a bright orange and red. It was blinding to look at but I couldn't take my eyes off of its beauty. The farther I got down the block, the bigger the houses got. These big three story houses with huge windows that you could look through and see these big gaudy chandeliers, or some other expensive accessory. All the houses were kept perfect, with either rocks or neatly cut grass on the front lawn that looked like it was professionally cut. I remember thinking how pretty everything was and comparing it to how ugly I felt. I felt such disgust because this wasn't me: wearing dresses, makeup, long hair. None of it was me.

That's when I realized the importance of what I was doing. It wasn't about a name, it was about becoming who I was truly meant to be. No matter what name I picked, it wouldn't change anything.

I knew who I was, and I knew what I needed to do. Maybe I was using not knowing a name as an excuse to put off actually coming out, but I had to do it. I would never be happy until I did it, until I said those words, "I'm a trans man." I said them a million times in my head, but never out loud, and that was a hard obstacle to overcome. I would try and practice when nobody was home. I'd go in the mirror and try to say it but I never could find the courage in me to bring it out. I knew it was there, I just had to take that leap of faith and let go. I was afraid of what people were going to think, but there comes a time where you need to put you and your priorities over other people's opinions.

When I got to the end of the street it was all open. There were two enormous houses, a tan one and a whitewashed grey one. They were on opposite sides of the street from each other, and directly in the middle was a small little pavilion with two benches and the rest was all open. I could smell the salt in the air, and the sky seemed so much bigger now that there wasn't anything blocking it's way. It opened up like a blooming flower with all these warm, beautiful, vibrant colors. For a split second, I felt like I wasn't on Earth anymore. It was like I was on this whole other planet with such a stunning view that I just couldn't move. It made me feel so good on the inside that I forgot all my problems. I wasn't worrying about the way I looked, or the way I felt, I was just in the moment.

After a couple minutes of zoning out, it felt abnormally quiet. Like I could hear the waves gently hitting the shore, and seagulls squawking above, but it felt like I was missing something. Like there was a noise before that was silenced now, and then I realized it was me. It was that little voice in the back of my head that was gone now. In those moments, I came to terms that this was who I was and I had no reason to be afraid or ashamed of it. I needed to own it and finally be myself. There was no little voice telling me to hide or lie. I had to do it now while I still had the courage in me.

I turned around, and I started walking back when I saw a lady walking her dog. As soon as she saw me, the dog started barking trying to come over to me, so the lady lightly pulled the chain to try and calm him down. However, somehow the chain must have gotten loose because the dog came running at me. I wasn't afraid or anything. In fact, I was laughing. He was a chocolate lab built really big. He came over and I started rubbing all down his side and behind his ears. His tail was wagging so fast it actually made a thumping noise as it hit my leg. Then the lady came running over. The poor thing was so embarrassed she didn't know what to do.

"I am so sorry!" she exclaimed.

"Don't be," I said chuckling.

"Ian, come here! Leave this young girl alone," she said to the dog.

She put the chain back on and continued with her walk. To her, that's all it was. She probably doesn't even remember that day, but I do. That's the day that changed my life. You see, I hadn't laughed or felt remotely happy for a very long time at that point in my life. Ian made me laugh, he made me smile, and so I decided that would be my name. I know it sounds stupid, and you probably wouldn't understand it, but you're not supposed to. That type of stuff is only supposed to make sense to me. It was my choice and that's what I wanted. I don't think I owe anyone an explanation as to why, or how, I came to that conclusion. I just went with what felt right, and in those moments, that's what I felt made the most sense.

After that walk, I went home and ate dinner, but I didn't talk much. I'm one of five kids so it's not like my silence was noticeable. I have two sisters, Kaylee and Alyssa, who were in eighth grade at the time and wouldn't stop talking about their big end of the year formal dance. It was the beginning of June, so everyone was starting to buy dresses, and our whole living room was filled with cutouts from magazines of dresses they wanted. My younger brother Jacob was nine. All he did was make fart jokes and complain about how gross Stephanie and her boyfriend were when they kissed. Stephanie is my older sister, who was super in love with this guy. The two of them made me gag because they never left each other's side. All they did was make out twenty-four seven. Lastly, was my little-older brother Ryan who was always a little different. I think that's why we got along the best out of all of my siblings. Ryan was quiet; he didn't talk about his life. He liked to keep his business personal, and I liked that about him. You never knew what was going on with him. He'd talk about his music or his art, but only if he was asked about it.

Anyways, I went the whole dinner trying to

build up the courage to say it out loud, but there wasn't a moment of silence. It was just one conversation to the next, and there was never even a second of a long pause for me to get a word in to change the subject. Finally, my mom asked me something. That was my chance to say it.

"Christine, can you pass me a napkin?" my mom asked.

"Ian," I replied.

She gave me a really confused look, and everyone else got quiet. Jacob laughed, but Rylee kicked him under the table.

"Ian?" she questioned.

"Yes," I answered.

"Christine, what is this about?" my father asked.

"Dad!" Ryan exclaimed.

"What?" he asked.

"Go ahead. Tell them Ian, it's about time," Ryan said to me.

How did Ryan know?

"What the hell is going on?" my dad questioned.

Now everyone was looking at me, expecting an explanation of what was going on, and there was Ryan, giving me a half smile.

"So, uh. You know how I'm a girl?" I asked.

Everyone just kept staring, needing more clarification as to what was going on.

"I, uh, um, I," I stuttered.

I had to pause and get myself together. I was getting so fluttered I couldn't even get my words together. Then, finally, I said it.

"I'm transgender. This whole girl thing, I can't do it. It's not me. My name is Ian and I want to be a boy," I came out with it.

Everyone looked shocked. They all just sat there, staring at me. So, I got up and went to my room. I figured they needed time to process it all. I wasn't even in the room a minute before Ryan came to check on me.

"That was brave and I'm proud of you," Ryan said.

"How'd you know?" I asked.

"Well, I didn't mean to, but one night while you were sleeping, I found your notebook on the floor. I was going to put it in your bag 'cause I thought it was from school, but when I opened it, I saw what it was about, so I just left it," he answered.

"Oh," I said.

"It wasn't on purpose, I swear. I just was trying to help, I," he went on.

"It's all good," I cut him off.

"Well, I guess I'll let you go," Ryan said.

"Wait. I was looking into it, and there's a doctor in Connecticut that's supposed to be really good. I'm thinking of going to consult with him," I told him.

"You're leaving?" he questioned.

"Not for long. Just a couple of weeks until I get stabilized on the right meds, then I'll be home again. Besides, I think everyone else needs time to work this through," I answered.

"I'm going to miss you," he said, hugging me really tight.

"Come with me," I said.

"Are you serious?" he asked.

"Yeah, you're eighteen. Mom and dad can't stop you," I replied.

"What about college?" Ryan asked.

"Take a year off like I did," I answered.

"You think it would be a good idea?" he questioned.

"I don't know, it's up to you. I don't want to force you, but I'm booking a bus ticket now, so if you want to come, start packing," I said.

"Why are you doing this?" he asked.

"Because everyone needs time to figure this whole thing out. I'm not even sure. I mean, I am sure this is what I want, but I have no idea what's in store for me, and I can't answer all their questions right now," I replied.

"So you're just going to run away?" Ryan asked.

"I'm coming back. I think it would just be better for now if everyone had some space," I answered.

"Then it's probably better if I stay here," he said.

"I didn't mean you," I reassured him.

"I know, but still, I think you need to do this on your own," Ryan said.

"You sure?" I asked one last time.

"Yeah," he said.

"I know you don't think it's a good idea, but I have to do this," I replied.

"Then go for it," he smiled.

After Ryan left the room, I packed my bag and walked back out to where everyone was sitting. Still in the same spots as before. I guess Ryan had told them what was going on because they didn't ask about the suitcase. They just all sat there with a confused look on their face. I didn't say good-bye or anything, I just turned and walked out. I knew my family well enough to know that if they disapproved of it, they would have been a lot more vocal. They were just confused, which I don't blame them, because I was too. I had no idea what this meant for me, but I knew this was the beginning of a new chapter.

It was six months later when I met Connor. I was on that same bus going back to see the same doctor for my six month check up. A lot had changed. I passed as a boy now, and I felt so much happier. I started to have stubble, and my voice was a little deeper, every day I felt like I kept growing into the man I was supposed to be. I was happy with my life, and who I was, and I don't think anyone could have changed that.

When Connor came on the bus and sat next to me, I was scared. He looked so sketchy to me. He was pale and really drawn. His hair was all messed up and he kept zoning out. He was just staring at one spot for like twenty minutes before shaking his head as he snapped out of whatever trance he was in. However, he was nice enough to give me a charger when my phone died, so I guess he had some decency in him.

When we came to my stop, we were the last

on the bus. He got up and darted off, leaving me behind to gather all my things. By the time I had all my things together and had made it off the bus, Connor was collapsed on the ground. I had no idea what happened, but I could tell it was something bad because he had broken down. I ran over to him. He was sobbing hysterically, and I tried to get him up, but he wasn't having it.

Nobody else was around that late at night, so I turned to tell the bus driver to call for help, but he had taken off, so it was just me. Cars passed us on the highway but they didn't care, they just buzzed right past us. I was totally baffled as to what to do, so I just got on the ground with him and tried to comfort him the best I could. I still had no idea what was going on. He was trying to tell me but he was so worked up that, between the tears and the gasping for air, none of it made sense.

Chapter 27

POV Connor

"Hello?" I questioned.

"Is this Connor?" the operator spoke.

"Yes," I said.

"Where are you now?" the operator asked.

"Who is this?" I asked back.

"Can you get to New York?" the operator questioned.

"New York?" I asked, confused.

"Yes," the operator said.

"I'm not even in New Jersey right now, I'm in Connecticut. Who is this?" I asked again.

"Look, there was an accident and we have your partner here. We need you to come pick up the belongings," the operator spoke.

"Alex? Is he okay?" I frantically questioned.

"I'm sorry but he passed away on impact. They tried to revive him on the site but it was too late," the operator said.

I hung up on her. I couldn't have been hearing that right. There was no way that this was real. It had to be fake. Someone was joking with me. No, it couldn't be happening. There was so much I wanted to say. There were still things we needed to work on. No, this wasn't happening, it couldn't have been happening. No, I wasn't ready to say goodbye. It had to be a joke. I was not ready. Why? Why was this happening to me? I didn't deserve any of this! None of it. I was not ready to live my life without him. I needed him and now he was gone. Why?

My phone started ringing again. It was the same number.

"Hello?" I picked it up.

"I'm not sure what happened, we got disconnected but," the operator began.

"What happened to Alex?" I demanded.

"We're still not sure how it happened, but there was an accident, and he was hit by a car. We did a toxicology report and he did have traces of cocaine in his system." the operator said.

"He's really gone? No! No, no, no, no, no. NOOOOO!" I yelled in agony.

"Please calm down," the operator said.

I was so mad that I just threw the phone at the ground. I didn't care that it shattered. I just couldn't believe it. Why was this happening to me? I had been fighting for so long, I couldn't handle another thing. This was just too much. It was way too much. I couldn't live without him. I didn't want to. I'd been fighting my whole life, and I was just falling apart. I'd lost everything one too many times. I was tired of starting over, and I couldn't convince myself that it would get better anymore. I didn't have an ounce of fight left in me, so I gave up entirely. That's when I felt a pair of hands grab mine.

I jumped because I thought I was alone. My eyes were so blurred that I couldn't make anything out. They burned so badly that when I rubbed them, it stung. Finally, I could make out what looked like a pair of small hands gently holding mine. I was able to finally make sense of what was going on. It was the kid from the bus.

I tried to tell him what was going on, but I couldn't. I was just so done. It was like I had everything I ever wanted and now it was gone. I waited so long to find someone like him. I can't tell you how many nights in the past I cried myself to sleep begging to find the one, and I thought I did. I thought I finally made it out of the dark, but I was wrong. It was all a false sense of hope. I didn't think it would ever get better. I begged God to end it all because I couldn't handle it. I didn't know what was going to come now that he was really gone. Even though we weren't together, I still told myself that maybe we'd work things out. Now, he was gone. I lost him and it was driving me crazy because there was nothing I could do to save my-self. I couldn't go back to being alone like I was before I met him. I couldn't picture the rest of my life without seeing him. It was all just too much.

I was so attached to him that he became a part of me. I was so used to calling him and talking to him. I still could picture it, and how safe I felt around him. He never had to do anything. Him just being there was always enough. Knowing I'd never see or feel that feeling again hurt me. It broke me to realize that he was really gone. There was no hope for us. There was no future like I pictured in my head. He was gone and there was nothing I could do about it. I still couldn't wrap my head around it.

How was I supposed to keep going when he was my everything? Before I met him, I was so lonely and insecure, but talking to him changed all that. I was mentally at my worst the night before I met him. It was five o'clock in the morning and I still couldn't sleep. All I could do was cry because I felt like such a screw up and a reject. I told myself that I would give life one last shot, and if it didn't get better, then I'd give up because there was no point in even trying if that's all my life was going to be. That next night I met him.

The second we started talking I felt something. I knew he was the one, and I still felt like he was. I mean he literally changed my life. How could I live without him? I loved him. I loved everything about him, and I wanted to give him the world because that's what he deserved. I was angry and sad, and I didn't know whether to scream or cry, so I did both. I wanted to just end it all. I didn't care, because I needed him. He was my life vest, and without him, I couldn't stay afloat.

All I could think about was how I was so sure he was the one. How happy I was that I didn't give up because it was all worth it, and now it was gone. It was gone! He was gone! I couldn't do it. I just wanted to not feel the pain I was feeling, but the more I tried to not think about it, the more it intensified. I just wanted to feel safe again. I wanted to laugh and smile like I did before, but that was all gone. Everything from before was gone. My life had just changed forever.

It's the worst feeling in the world to have everything taken away from you, especially when there is nothing you can do about it. That sense of feeling trapped eats you alive. When you have the motivation to want to get better, and you really put the effort into trying to make things work, but the world just keeps knocking you down. Each time you get up, it's harder and harder. Eventually, the physical work you have to put into getting up everyday actually isn't worth the pain you get for trying, so you just give up because you know it's not getting better.

I remember being so mad at God, at the world, even at myself. It felt like I had lost everything and everyone had given up on me. I couldn't cry anymore, so I just sat there, looking up at the dark night sky. There was one star in the whole sky and the rest was pitch black and cloudy. So cloudy that you couldn't even see the moon, it was just a blur of light that was covered by clouds. I looked up at that star and I begged whatever power above was in control of things to please help me. I couldn't do it anymore. Was I really that bad of a person that I deserved all that? I didn't think so. All I ever wanted to do was help others. I didn't know any of the answers, and it made me mad, because if I was doing something wrong, I wanted to know so I could fix it.

I sat there waiting for a sign, something, anything to tell me it was going to be okay, but nothing. Just the sound of cars passing by on the highway.

"You okay?" Ian asked.

"You're still here?" I asked back.

"Yeah. This is my stop, and when I saw what happened, I figured you might need someone," he said.

"I don't need you, I need Alex," I said.

"Who's Alex? Can I call him?" Ian asked.

"You don't get it! He's gone!" I laughed.

"Oh," he said.

"Yeah, so there is no help for me," I said.

"Don't say that," Ian tried to reassure me.

"Really. I just lost the only person to ever make me feel happy, and I'll never know what that feels like again. It's all gone! I hate it here! I'M SO DONE! WHY? WHY DID YOU DO THIS TO ME?" I started to scream.

"Look, why don't you come to my hotel with me and we can figure this out," Ian said.

"No, I can't. I have to get to New York," I demanded.

"New York is a couple hours drive away from here. You aren't getting there tonight," he said.

"I have to!" I exclaimed.

"Well at least let's get an hour's rest before we go," Ian said.

"We?" I asked.

"I'm not going to let you do this alone," he tried to console me.

"I don't need your help," I replied.

"Fine, but the next bus doesn't come until five," he said.

He started walking away, and even though I wanted to be alone, I dreaded it because I knew nothing good would come from it. I needed a sound minded person to keep me from spiraling.

"Wait," I caved.

He turned around as if he knew exactly what I was about to say. I got up and the both of us walked over to the diner to get something to eat before going back to the hotel.

When we walked in, the place was empty with one waitress on staff managing the bar and the tables. She was behind the bar cleaning out a beer glass with one of those white rags when she looked up to see us and brought us to our seats. We sat at a booth, all the way in the back, next to one of the windows which was fogging up from the heat inside and the cold outside. I wasn't that hungry, so I just ordered juice, but Ian ordered pancakes.

"When we get to the hotel, I'll see if they have a rental car place so we can leave. Did they give you an address?" Ian questioned.

"No. I still don't even know how he ended up in New York," I replied.

"Well hopefully they'll have some answers for you," he said.

"So what brings you all the way to the middle of nowhere?" I asked, trying to change the topic.

By now, our order was there. Now that I had some caffeine in my system, I felt a little less dead tired, but with that came a ton of nervous energy that I was trying to contain. However, I slowly felt myself losing my grip. I wanted to be in New York already. I wanted to know what happened. I wanted this whole thing to be done and over with. Ian was talking, but I kind of zoned him out while I tried to get a hold of myself. I took several deep breaths and tried to tell myself that Alex was gone.

I couldn't change that or let that destroy me. I was still here. I still had a life to live. I couldn't stop it though, so I just got up and walked out, leaving Ian there. I didn't care if he was being nice, I just needed answers.

"Where are you going? Wait holdup!" Ian said.

I was already out the door before he could even catch up to me. I needed to know what happened. At most, I just needed some closure. I couldn't stop my mind from going through all these different scenarios, and it just would have helped to know for sure.

Chapter 28
POV Ian

My heart broke for Connor. I didn't know him that well, but I could tell he was hurting. I wanted to comfort him, but I felt the best thing I could do was let him get it all out. I know from my own personal experiences that bottling up your emotions never ends well. So, I sat there with him, watching him cry, yell, scream, and cry again. All the while, I just wanted to give him a really big hug. I know that's what comforts me when I'm feeling down and out, but I didn't want to hug him 'cause I was a total stranger and I felt like that was crossing a line. So I just sat there, and when it was finally over, I tried to talk to him.

I couldn't figure out exactly what was going on at first, but finally, he was starting to make sense. Alex, who I thought was his boyfriend, was in an accident and he needed to go to New York to pick up his things. How he was getting to New York was beyond me. Not only was it the middle of the night, he was in no mental condition to do it alone. So, I offered my company. At first, he rejected it so I walked away, but I knew he would take me up on my offer. Nobody willingly chooses to be alone.

I told him it would be better if we put something in our stomachs before we went back to my hotel to rest and see if they had a rental car service. While we were waiting for our food, I emailed my doctor and told him I'd have to reschedule, which wasn't a big deal. It had happened in the past where I couldn't make the appointment. They would probably just bill me a twenty dollar cancellation fee and I'd have to call to reschedule. It was no big deal. I had been on Testosterone long enough to know what I was doing. There wasn't anything he was going to tell me that I didn't already know.

I was trying to distract him, but I didn't know what to talk about. I was trying to think of something, but it was hard because I didn't really know him. In fact, I knew nothing about him. He was a stranger. I didn't know what we had in common, or what he liked, so I just went with music. Everyone loves music. The place had an old jukebox that was playing 80's music, so I started there, hoping we'd be able to build a conversation off of that.

"So, you listen to music a lot?" I asked.

He didn't answer.

"Connor?" I questioned.

Still, he didn't acknowledge me. I could tell he was zoning out because he was looking right at me, but he had a really blank stare on his face. Looking at his eyes, I could see they were empty on the inside, and he just sat there perfectly still. I didn't want to snap him out of it because I knew he was probably trying to figure out and sort through all his feelings. I couldn't even imagine being in his position and losing someone that close to me, so I figured it was best to let him work it all out.

It was like that for about ten minutes before he

just got up and walked out. I tried to stop him, but whatever he was doing, he had his mind made up. I took my wallet and threw two twenty dollar bills down on the table and ran after him. By the time I made it out there, he had vanished.

"Connor?" I yelled, "Connor?"

I was listening carefully, maybe to hear his footsteps or something, but it was dead silent. I tried to think, where would he go? New York. He was at the bus stop, and sure enough, when I got there, he was standing there waiting very impatiently.

"There aren't any more buses until the morning," I said.

"It's fine, I can wait," Connor replied.

"Will you just come back to the hotel with me? I can help you, don't push me away," I pleaded.

"Look, I don't even know you and I'm supposed to trust you?" he questioned.

"I know you don't know me, but right now, who do you have?" I asked.

He just kind of sat there for a second, looking around. I could tell by his face that he was realizing how alone he truly was.

"I still don't know you," Connor said.

"My name is Ian. I'm trans, and my dead-name

is Christine, which my dad still calls me because when he looks at me, he still sees his daughter. My older sister is married with a baby that I'm not allowed to see because she's afraid I'll turn it gay. My mom hasn't been able to look me in the eye since I came out. Is that enough?" I asked.

"Look, I'm sorry, but you still can't help me," he replied.

"Then talk to me! Tell me what I can do, but whatever you do, just don't try and do this alone!" I exclaimed.

"What are you like crazy or something? Do you have an obsession with me or something?" Connor asked.

"No?" I questioned.

"Then why are you still here?" he asked.

"Because when I look at you, I see someone who is broken. So broken that they can barely keep it together. You think you're good at hiding it, but I see right through it. On the outside you act all tough, pushing everyone who tries to help you away, but on the inside, a small part of you that you've buried so deep down wants them to stay. But you don't want to face that reality because you can't accept the fact that this is all too much for you. You think it makes you weak, but you're not weak. You just lost someone you loved. It's okay to be upset. You're not weak for having feelings," I said.

He sat there for about two minutes, not saying a word. He looked shocked, as if to say "how the hell did he know all that?" but he didn't see himself the way the rest of the world did. He was trying to convince himself so hard that he was winning the fight, but just looking at him, you could tell he had reached his limit a long time ago. I didn't want to burst his bubble, but someone had to tell him that there comes a time when you need to ask for help. He needed to know that there was nothing wrong with asking for help. That it takes more courage and bravery to step up and say "I can't handle this, I need help," than it does to try and fake it.

"You just don't understand," Connor said.

"Was I wrong?" I asked.

"No, but it's not that simple. There's so much more and you just don't understand," he answered.

"Then help me," I said.

"Help you what?" he asked.

"Understand. Talk to me. You can vent, I'm here for you," I said back.

Chapter 29
POV Connor

When Ian started explaining what he saw to me, it was actually almost scary because everything he said was true. I was broken. I needed so much help, but my problem was that I wanted someone else to fix it. I wanted someone else to walk into my life and make everything go away. Reality was, I had to fix it myself. I had to be strong. Although I missed Alex, I didn't need him. I didn't need a boyfriend to be happy. The only thing I needed was to accept myself, and I just couldn't do that. There was so much ugly about me. The things I'd been through, I felt ashamed of them, but in those moments, I knew that I couldn't be. I had to take all the things that tried to break me and turn them into power. I had to turn all that negative energy into motivation to do better.

I put all my time and energy into focusing on a boyfriend because I felt like that's what I needed to make me happy. The truth is, you can make yourself happy on your own. It starts with loving yourself and doing the things that give you fulfill-ment in life. You have to believe in yourself and want to do better. A partner doesn't validate you, and that was a lesson I needed to learn. I spent so much time focusing on how lonely I was and how I wanted a boyfriend to make things better, but I didn't need that.

I needed to learn to be happy with myself. I needed to love my flaws, my imperfections, and learn that everything about me was perfect. It's about knowing your worth and not wasting your time on people who don't deserve you just because it's better to have somebody than nobody. Al-though I'm convinced Alex was the love of my life, I would need to learn to live without him because there was nothing he brought me that I couldn't do for myself.

I am a gay man and that is okay. I have done some stupid things in my past: lying, self harming, drinking, just to name a few. None of that makes me a bad person, because no matter the mistake, big or small, as long as you learn from it and fix it, you're on the right path. In today's world, it is so hard to win everyone's acceptance. You'll never be happy if you keep trying to find your own validation in other people. The only time you'll ever be truly happy is when you finally stand up to the bullies and the haters out there and be fearlessly you. I was just finding that out.

I was just finding out that I didn't need to be ashamed of anything because it didn't matter what people thought of me. I'd never be happy if I kept that mindset. I had to be me or else I'd never find my inner peace and acceptance.

"Where do you want me to start?" I asked.

"From the beginning," Ian replied.

"It all started on Saturday, April 13th."

Book Summary

Connor, and Alex are two young gay men who had both given up on the idea of love. Whether it be toxic exes who broke their trust, or just not having any luck finding that person that they really connected with, it had just taken a toll on the both of them. Neither of them went into that bar with the intention of anything other than getting drunk, but somehow walked out sober and the happiest they'd both been in a long time.

From the very beginning it was an instant connection, and they both knew that they'd finally done it, they finally found "the one". Together they laughed, cried, and smiled together, building the dream life they'd always wanted. Once you start to read their story you'll find yourself gasping, crying, and even smiling, because that's what true love is. There's a lot of emotion put into loving someone, and Connor and Alex learned this firsthand.